William Marshall

The Passion of Christ

REFLECTIONS ON
THE GOOD FRIDAY REPROACHES

THE COLUMBA PRESS • APCK

First edition, 1997, published by
THE COLUMBA PRESS
55A Spruce Avenue, Stillorgan Industrial Park,
Blackrock, Co Dublin
and
APCK
St Ann's Bookcentre, Dawson Street, Dublin 2

ISBN 1 85607 184 7

Cover by Bill Bolger
Origination by The Columba Press
Printed in Ireland by Colour Books Ltd, Dublin

Acknowledgements
The English translation of the Reproaches from the *Rite of Holy Week* copyright © 1972, International Committee on English in the Liturgy Inc. All rights reserved.

Reproduction on the cover of *Ecce Homo* by Titian, courtesy of the National Gallery of Ireland.

Contents

For Margaret

The Reproaches

I

My people, what have I done to you?
How have I offended you? Answer me!

I led you out of Egypt, from slavery to freedom,
but you led your Saviour to the cross.

My people, what have I done to you?
How have I offended you? Answer me!

Holy is God!
Holy and strong!
Holy and immortal One,
have mercy on us!

For forty years I led you safely through the desert.
I fed you with manna from heaven
and brought you to a land of plenty;
but you led your Saviour to the cross.

Holy is God!
Holy and strong!
Holy and immortal One,
have mercy on us!

What more could I have done for you?
I planted you as my fairest vine,
but you yielded only bitterness:
when I was thirsty you gave me vinegar to drink,
and you pierced your Saviour with a lance.

Holy is God!
Holy and strong!
Holy and immortal One,
have mercy on us!

II

For your sake I scourged your captors and their firstborn sons,
but you brought your scourges down on me.

My people, what have I done to you?
How have I offended you? Answer me!

I led you from slavery to freedom
and drowned your captors in the sea,
but you handed me over to your high priests.

My people, what have I done to you?
How have I offended you? Answer me!

I opened the sea before you,
but you opened my side with a spear.

My people, what have I done to you?
How have I offended you? Answer me!

I led you on your way in a pillar of cloud,
but you led me to Pilate's court.

My people, what have I done to you?
How have I offended you? Answer me!

I bore you up with manna in the desert,
but you struck me down and scourged me.

My people, what have I done to you?
How have I offended you? Answer me!

I gave you saving water from the rock,
but you gave me gall and vinegar to drink.

My people, what have I done to you?
How have I offended you? Answer me!

For you I struck down the kings of Canaan,
but you struck my head with a reed.

My people, what have I done to you?
How have I offended you? Answer me!

I gave you a royal sceptre,
but you gave me a crown of thorns.

My people, what have I done to you?
How have I offended you? Answer me!

I raised you up to the height of majesty,
but you raised me high on a cross.

My people, what have I done to you?
How have I offended you? Answer me!

Introduction

'Crucified under Pontius Pilate'. The very familiarity of this phrase from the Apostles' Creed may disguise from modern people its truly shocking character. It states that Jesus Christ, the one whom Christians worship as God's supreme revelation of himself, was put to death as a condemned criminal in a particularly cruel and shameful way. The Roman author Cicero stated, 'Let even the name of the cross be kept away not only from the bodies of the citizens of Rome, but also from their thought, sight and hearing.' Yet Christians not only admit that their Lord and Master died on a cross, they glory in that fact and find in it the basis of their relationship with God.

Over the centuries Christians have struggled to grasp and express what the suffering of Christ means to them in their life as his disciples who know themselves to be accepted by God through him. What God has done through Christ's cross is a fact of stupendous significance which will always be greater than any attempt to explain its meaning. It communicates to people at a level deeper and simpler than the understanding, and Christians have learnt to worship and adore the crucified Lord before they can explain in words how the cross brings them to God. They have preferred to use the language of awe, thanksgiving, repentance and self-committal to that of theological exposition when they speak about the cross. Sometimes words of any kind fail and they have taken refuge in silence and in actions. Looking at a crucifix or a crown of thorns, carrying a wooden cross in procession, or going in imagination through the events of Holy Week, have helped people in every age to enter into the meaning of Christ's passion and let it shape their lives. Intellectual puzzling over the reasons for and the effects of the crucifixion can both help and be helped by the more primary activity of dwelling on the event itself.

In Christian history many different devotional forms have arisen which fix attention on the mystery of Christ's suffering. This rich treasury includes many passion hymns, the three hours devotion on the seven words from the cross, the stations of the cross, the sorrowful mysteries of the rosary, as well as pilgrimages and processions of witness. Books have been written to expound these devotions and help people use them in their own spiritual life. One devotion, the Reproaches, has not, as far as I know, received any extensive treatment in book form and I hope, in the following pages, to see what light it sheds on Christ's redemption through the cross, and how it may help to bring home to us this central fact of our faith.

The Reproaches, sometimes referred to by their Latin title *Improperia*, have long been familiar to Roman Catholics as part of the Mass of the Presanctified on Good Friday (the Mass without the consecration prayer but with communion from previously consecrated elements). The Reproaches are a distinct and detachable form of prayer within the structure of the Mass, and in recent years have been increasingly used as part of their Good Friday worship by several churches. Good Friday is a suitable day for ecumenical services and in many areas Christians come together for joint acts of witness and worship, often including a procession carrying a cross from the church of one denomination to that of another, with united services in both places. The Reproaches are one of the many acts of devotion which could be, and no doubt are, prayed on such occasions.

The Joint Liturgical Group, representing several denominations in England, published a book entitled *Holy Week Services* in 1971, with an enlarged edition in 1983, which contained a version of the Reproaches. A different version appeared in the Church of England publication *Lent, Holy Week, Easter* in 1984. The Anglican Church of Canada in its *Book of Alternative Services* (1985) has also a modern version of the Reproaches. It is interesting to note that Dorothy L. Sayers used the format of the Reproaches to good effect as Mary Magdalene's lamentation at the cross in her play cycle on Christ's life, *The Man Born to be King*. The structure of the main part of the Reproaches lends itself readily to this kind of adaptation. God is represented as addressing his people, contrasting his care of them through history with the way they treated Christ.

I led you out of Egypt, from slavery to freedom,
but you led your Saviour to the cross.

This framework allows us to contrast any of God's gracious deeds with any of the innumerable crimes of humanity.

The Reproaches were probably composed in the ninth century in France or Spain. They were written in Latin but included an earlier Greek hymn, the *Trisagion*, 'Holy is God ...', which was an entrance chant in the Orthodox liturgy from the fifth century. The Reproaches formed part of the ceremony of the Veneration of the Cross. After the Roman Emperor Constantine made Christianity a legal religion, and adopted it himself, Christians were able to practise their faith openly, and they would naturally take an interest in the holy places where our Lord had lived and walked on earth. Jerusalem became a place of pilgrimage and the forms of worship there set standards for the rest of the Christian world. In particular, the celebration of Holy Week and Easter in Jerusalem would influence worship in other places. The Emperor's mother, St Helena, made a pilgrimage to Jerusalem and, according to legend, found the true cross on which our Saviour died. Even apart from this belief, it is natural that Jerusalem would evoke vivid awareness of Christ's death as a physical event. Pilgrims would know they were standing on the ground where Christ spent his last night on earth, where he prayed with agony in the garden, where he was betrayed, arrested and denied, condemned to death, mocked, flogged, crucified and buried. The ceremonies at Jerusalem were adapted and copied in other places. If a particular church had what was claimed to be a relic of the true cross, that would be greatly prized but, in any case, the use of a material cross would aid devotion. A rough, unadorned, wooden cross placed before the Good Friday worshippers is a powerful reminder of the brutal fact of the crucifixion. To touch a wooden cross is to begin to know at a physical level the hard earthy event which is our Saviour's death for us.

The sight of the cross and the words of the Reproaches combine very effectively to show the significance of Christ's passion. The repeated words 'You led your Saviour to the cross' hold our attention on what Christ did and suffered. The main part of the Reproaches is a series of statements in which God and Jesus address the worshippers in words which promote heart-searching and repentance. But they are not purely inward-looking or guilt-inducing. 'The triumph of the Cross, the anguish of the Crucified, and the responsibility of the people are all represented' (J. D. Crichton in *A Manual for Holy Week*, ed. C. P. M. Jones, p. 30).

The Reproaches usually contain four parts, which can vary in order. In the first, God challenges his people to respond to his loving care of them in contrast to their treatment of the Saviour. The people answer, 'Holy is God! Holy and strong! Holy and immortal One, have mercy on us!' In the second and longest part, God lists his mighty saving deeds for his people and contrasts each of them with various aspects of Christ's sufferings. (Sometimes the term 'Reproaches' is used for this part alone.) The third and shortest part (which sometimes comes first), is an antiphon in praise of Christ's cross and resurrection. The final section is a hymn of triumph, most frequently *Pange lingua gloriosi*, 'Sing my tongue the glorious battle'. The Reproaches place the horror and guilt of human sin, so clearly revealed by the crucifixion, in the setting of God's great rescue act of the human race through the victory of Christ's cross.

In Christian thought, Christ's death can never be simply a tragedy, the defeat of right by might, the sad end of a beautiful life. The death itself is a victory which is clearly revealed in the resurrection. The sense of the cross as triumph in no way reduces the horror, pain, shame and dereliction Christ endured for us. Christ became weak, vulnerable, the victim of evil, and it is precisely in his submission to the power of evil forces that his victory lies. St Paul writes, 'He was crucified in weakness, but lives by the power of God' (2 Cor 13:4). The central Christian truth is that Christ suffered death and rose again. In the early church, the crucifixion and resurrection were celebrated together as the Christian Passover, the paschal mystery. With the development of the church's year after Constantine, the different events in Christ's saving work were separated out and celebrated in turn. But none was seen in isolation from the total work of God. Christians could not celebrate Good Friday without remembering that it is followed by Easter Day. There was a tendency, particularly in the Western church, to emphasise the passion of Christ in its details – the agony in the garden, the scourging, the crown of thorns and, above all, the long drawn out suffering on the cross. This particular Western emphasis continued after the

Reformation equally among Protestants and Roman Catholics. Great passion hymns like 'When I survey the wondrous cross' breathe the same spirit of devotion as the use of a crucifix. The Reproaches as a Good Friday devotion belong clearly to this Western tradition in their emphasis on Christ's sufferings and sorrow for our sins which brought him to the cross. Along with passiontide hymns and other devotions, they can be deeply moving in their appeal to our hearts and minds as we contemplate all that Christ has done for us. We need not regard them in a mawkish or sentimental way or as a neurotic wallowing in guilt. They can be a highly appropriate response of the whole person – understanding, emotions and will – to the mystery of the cross. Perhaps the title, 'Reproaches', isolates one element in this devotion, sorrow for our sins which caused Christ's suffering, whereas the act as a whole is a celebration of God's mighty work of salvation in Christ, of which our penitence forms only one, though an essential, part. Some modern versions do not use the title 'Reproaches'. The English *Lent, Holy Week, Easter* version is called 'The proclamation of the cross' and the Canadian book has 'Meditation on the Cross of Jesus'. However, there is no generally accepted title other than 'the Reproaches' which I shall therefore continue to use.

Two further issues may raise questions about the Reproaches for modern people. They have been thought to be anti-Jewish, as implying that the Jews were especially guilty for the crucifixion, and for this reason some places have given up using them in their Good Friday worship. They also, in a few verses, portray an Old Testament view of God taking vengeance on Israel's enemies, as in the words 'For your sakes I scourged your captors and their first-born sons ...' I shall deal with the second problem in a later chapter. Regarding the alleged anti-Jewish character of the Reproaches, J. D. Crichton writes:

> Some have mistakenly supposed that these 'reproaches' are addressed to the Jews. The perspective is quite different. The fathers of the church saw the People of God as a whole, their history reaching back into the Old Testament, finding its fulfilment in the New and represented in the Church of today. In these texts Christ is envisaged as hanging on the cross addressing words of reproach to the whole human race who bear responsibility for bringing him to the cross. But they are

words too that seek a change of heart, conversion (*Manual of Holy Week*, p.30).

The Reproaches have some resemblance to the Jewish devotion *Dayenu*, used in the Passover liturgy in which a number of God's mighty acts in creating, saving and caring for his people are recounted, but there is no need to regard the Reproaches as 'reproaching' the Jews in particular with ingratitude to God for his past goodness to them. In view of the shameful record of Christian persecution of Jews over the centuries, it needs to be emphatically stated that all the sins of all the human race brought Jesus to the cross. It would be a pity if the great devotional value of the Reproaches were to be lost through the mistaken supposition that they are anti-Jewish. In fact they 'reproach' all of us in the manner of Old Testament prophets pleading with God's people to repent and return to him. The Canadian version of the Reproaches corrects any possible misunderstanding when it includes the verse:

I grafted you into the tree of my chosen Israel,
and you turned on them with persecution and mass murder.
I made you joint heirs with them of my covenants,
but you made them scapegoats for your own guilt.
Holy God, holy and mighty,
holy and immortal one, have mercy upon us.

The Reproaches form a meditation on the different events which befell Christ during his passion. In their traditional form, some event in the story of God's care for his people recorded in the Old Testament is contrasted with a New Testament reference to the passion narrative, as 'I led you on your way in a pillar of cloud, but you led me to Pilate's court'.

New Testament scholars stress the importance of preaching in the formation of the four gospels, as Christ's words and actions were proclaimed many times to the early believers before anything was written down. Hence the sayings and deeds of Jesus are frequently grouped according to topic rather than in order of occurrence, which in any case can differ from gospel to gospel. But the passion of Christ had the supreme place in Christian preaching from the very beginning, and, in the words of a major New Testament scholar, Raymond E. Brown, the passion narrative 'constitutes in each gospel the longest consecutive action recounted of Jesus' (*The Death of the Messiah*, p.vii. I am deeply indebted to this authoritative, two-volume work in what follows, though I make no attempt at New Testament scholarship). The earliest gospel, Mark, has a very long section, in proportion to the whole, which deals with the last week of Christ's life on earth and much of it relates the events of the last twenty-four hours, reflecting its importance for early Christian preaching. Yet the first believers were not merely concerned with fact but with meaning for Christian living and for understanding of who Christ really is. The historic fact of Christ's death by crucifixion is essential to the truth of Christianity. Hence, while the early preachers related what happened in and around Jerusalem at that Passover time, their concern was not with verifiable details, like that of a modern newspaper reporter, but with the importance for faith of Christ's actions and suffering. The clause 'Suffered under Pontius Pilate' in the creed roots Christ's death in secular history and no serious thinker doubts its historic truth. The evangelists relate what actually happened with a particular purpose in mind and not as neutral recorders of events. The concern of the Reproaches is similar; they are based entirely on the Bible and portray the events of the passion as the outworking of the divine plan. It is probably impossible to go behind the evangelists' records to all the factual details, but we have in the gospels a factually based understanding of God's mighty act of salvation in Christ, and it is in that spirit that I shall consider the various events of the passion narratives in the following pages. Thus I shall not deal, for example, with the historical and critical problem of whether Christ was crucified at 'the third hour', 9.00 am, as St Mark states (15:25), although according to St John he stood before Pilate 'about noon' (19:14). The truth for Christian faith of Christ's great work on the cross is what matters and not the precise sequence of events, though the basic historic fact is necessary for belief with integrity and it is not seriously questioned by historians.

In the chapters which follow, I shall take the main events of the passion story as a basis for considering our Lord's great work on the cross, with the help of the insights found in the words of the Reproaches. This work is not a commentary on the Reproaches, nor is it as closely connected to them as my previous book, *O Come, Emmanuel*, was to the Advent Antiphons. The Reproaches do not readily lend themselves to that kind of treatment. They are more a structure which can be widely adapted to different concerns than a fixed form. Their great value, however, is that, like the gospels themselves on which they are fully based, they interpret Christ's passion for us and enable us to respond to it with our whole selves.

CHAPTER 1

A Passionate God

What is God like?

Everyone has some idea of what the word 'God' means, even if they do not believe there is a God or gods. Belief in one God, one supreme being, is widespread among the world's peoples, even if it coexists with worship of a number of lesser gods or spirits. While there are different conceptions of this one God, certain basic ideas are to be found in the world's main religions. God is beyond human thought yet human beings can enter into relationship with him. (I use masculine pronouns to refer to the one God in accordance with universal usage until recent years, fully accepting its limited, analogical sense.) We attribute to God the highest and best qualities we can find – he is good, loving, all-powerful, eternal – yet are aware that these words can only hint at, not describe adequately, what he is.

Christians believe that the fullest revelation of God's nature is found in the life and teaching of Jesus Christ. Jesus was a Jew, born and nurtured in the Jewish religion, and his work and message cannot be understood apart from their Jewish context. His revelation of God was not totally new but fulfilled God's revelation through the Jewish people. The Jewish Bible, which Christians call the Old Testament, is of great importance for the Christian understanding of God. For both Jews and Christians it is the authoritative, foundational document against which to test statements about God, though for Christians it has to be understood in relation to its fulfilment in Christ as shown in the New Testament. Christians use the words and ideas of the Old Testament very frequently to describe Christ's saving work, as in the Good Friday Reproaches. Yet for Christians, the words and example of Christ have higher authority than the Old Testament. They give a fuller and deeper insight into God's nature and correct some aspects of the Old Testament portrayal of God. Are there any other ways than the Jewish and Christian scriptures by which we can know about God? The first Christians clearly thought there were. Reason, experience, observation, conscience can all give us some notion of what God is like. When Paul and Barnabas were talking to the people of Lystra in Asia Minor they said that God 'did not leave himself without witness, for he did good and gave you from heaven rain and fruitful seasons, satisfying your hearts with food and gladness' (Acts 14:17). As Christianity spread in the Roman Empire, where Greek philosophy had a dominant influence on human thought, many Christian teachers used the concepts and beliefs of their hearers in which to express and commend the Christian faith. The second century apologist Justin Martyr thought of some of the Greek philosophers as 'Christians before Christ'. Even a writer like Tertullian, who considered non-Christian thought of little value, used the thought-forms of his culture, in particular the terms *persona* and *substantia,* to develop the doctrine of the Trinity. Every preacher and evangelist has to begin where people are. He must build on the existing knowledge and concepts of his hearers to get his message across, though he may have to correct their mistakes and will inevitably go beyond their presuppositions. Christianity took shape in the world of Greek and Roman thought and this setting deeply affected not only the terms they used to speak about God but also Christian ideas about God's nature.

The Greeks and Romans worshipped many gods but at the time of Christ the more thoughtful among them were not satisfied with the traditional stories of the often disreputable doings of gods and godesses and hankered after a religion of ethical purity and a God to whom they could with integrity give their allegiance. They were attracted by the Jewish belief in one unseen God who is distinct from the created world and anything in it and who is morally good and requires right behaviour from his worshippers. Philosophers such as Aristotle taught that God must be above all human frailty and unaffected by anything in this world. The prevalent Greek idea was that God inhabits the world of being, static perfection, whereas this world is one of 'becoming', change and decay, growth and death. God is the 'Unmoved Mover' who draws creation to himself by the power of his goodness but is not contaminated by this changing, messy scene. God is 'impassible', not able to suffer, which would be untrue to his divine nature.

In many ways, Greek thought enriched Christian understanding. It drew out truths implicit in the Bible and gave philosophic terms by which to develop and commend the Christian faith in the world of the Roman Empire. The Greek ideas about God do not contradict the Bible, but there is a different feeling and atmosphere between the two. In particular, the thought that God is impassible has a very different outlook from the portrayal of God who yearns with love for his often troublesome people, as found in both Old and New Testaments. Greek thought warns us against making God in our own image by ascribing to him human feelings with all their defects, and the Bible does exactly the same. The God of the Bible, like the God of the Greek philosophers, is very different from human beings. But whereas the Greeks expressed the difference in abstract and negative terms, the biblical authors did so by stressing the authority, sovereignty and lordship of God. The Greeks concentrate on what God is not, the negative way of speaking about him. The Bible shows us what God is like, the way of analogy. When we say that God loves us, we are claiming that God's love has some resemblance to human love but is without the limitations of human love. The great advantage of the biblical way of speaking is that it conveys a very full, rich and positive awareness of God. The danger of speaking in these vigorous terms is anthropomorphism, making God in the form of man, thinking of him as merely a magnified version of ourselves. The safeguard against this danger is to remember the limitations of all human words in speaking about God. The commandments warn of this danger when they forbid us to worship anything but God or any image of God.

> You shall not make for yourself an idol, whether in the form of anything that is in heaven above, or that is on the earth beneath, or that is in the water under the earth. You shall not bow down to them nor worship them (Ex 20:4-5).

If we understand this commandment correctly as forbidding the worship of all images as God, including all ideas of God in limited, human language, then we can safely take the vigorous anthropomorphic terms of the Bible as bringing us into living contact with the living God. Indeed it is essential to do so for the full truth of God. The abstract terms of philosophy – impassible, pure being, without body or parts – may mislead us into thinking that we have a true and adequate idea of God, whereas their main function is to show us what God is not, and to direct our attention away from the world of finite objects to the all-surpassing reality.

How the Bible speaks of God

The very simplicity and humanity of the Bible's words about God, who walked in the garden in the cool of the day (Gen 3:8) and 'came down to see the city and tower which mortals had built' (Gen 11:5), protect us from the absurdity of understanding them literally while, at the same time, they convey the personal reality of the living God that would be lost were we to attempt to translate them into abstract terms. The words of the Bible do not simply give us information about God but communicate more deeply than that. In their total impact they touch our feelings and will; they can change our outlook and how we behave. Their value lies in that they do not just tell us *about* God, but enable us in some sense to come into contact with God. Why do we read the Bible over and over again, publicly in church according to a lectionary and privately by whatever scheme we choose? No doubt we need to remind ourselves of what we may have forgotten, but the Christmas and Easter stories, for example, are very well known, yet those festivals would not be complete without them. We read them, not for new information but to nourish our spirits by hearing again in wonder and thanksgiving the mighty acts God has done for love of his human family.

Children, in their attitude to their favourite stories, understand this truth instinctively. They want to hear a story they may know off by heart, over and over again. They howl in protest if one detail is changed. A logical but stupid adult might argue, 'What does it matter if Little Red Riding Hood were named Little Blue Riding Hood, wore a blue cloak and visited her aunt at the lake side rather than her grandmamma in the forest?' Children know better. They have entered into the world of the story, it is real to them and the specific details of people, place, sight and sound all make up the authentic experience of hearing the story. The Bible, like other literature of enduring value, nourishes the human spirit by its total impact and while it needs to be interpreted, summarised and its essential teaching expounded in systematic form, no summary or explanation is a substitute for the Bible itself.

The Bible's presentation of God in very human terms, as well as its stress on God's infinite difference from human beings, needs to be fully appreciated by all who wish to be open to the reality of the God to whom it bears witness. God is shown in the Bible as loving his people with passionate yearning. He is often moved to sorrow at their disobedience to his commands, which are for their true happiness. He is represented as jealous and angry when they follow self-chosen ways which he knows can only bring disaster upon them. He is impatient with them, exasperated and disappointed. He expostulates with them, pleads for their return to his love and protection and he is willing to go to any lengths to bring that about.

This way of portraying God, particularly in the Old Testament, clearly reflects the human limitations of the biblical authors. In some passages God sounds very like an angry father who needs to be pacified and persuaded not to be too hard on his erring children. When the people of Israel worshipped the golden calf we read:

> The LORD said to Moses, 'I have seen this people, how stiff-necked they are. Now let me alone, so that my wrath may burn hot against them and I may consume them …' But Moses implored the LORD his God and said, 'O LORD, why does your wrath burn hot against your people, whom you brought out of the land of Egypt with great power and with a mighty hand?… Turn from your fierce wrath; change your mind and do not bring disaster on your people …' And the LORD changed his mind about the disaster that he planned to bring on his people (Ex 32:9-14).

There is something here of the irascible Victorian father storming into the house, making everyone shake in their shoes, but also amenable to the calming words of his wife or a respected servant who can talk him round to a more gentle frame of mind. It would be blasphemous to attribute either quality to God in any straightforward sense. 'For my thoughts are not your thoughts, nor are your ways my ways, says the LORD' (Isa 55:8). 'God is not a human being that he should lie, or a mortal that he should change his mind' (Num 23:19). God does not share our human imperfections and limitations. The Greeks were right to insist that he is 'without passions', if passions are understood as uncontrolled emotions which influence his attitudes and actions.

But both his love and his anger, understood in an analogical sense, point to a quality in God which Greek abstractions fail to convey. Perhaps we come closest to a true understanding of God's anger if we think of a parent's worry over the behaviour of a child who disobediently runs into danger. In such cases a father or mother's language can show a lack of logic matched only by the depths of its concern. 'If you run out on that road again I'll kill you! Don't you know you might get killed?!' A child's healthy fear of his parents' anger can be a necessary protection when growing up. The passionate language of the Old Testament about God's anger must be understood not as exactly like human anger but as bearing some resemblance to it. This way of speaking cannot be given up if we are to know the real God.

Christ's Portrayal of God

The New Testament also presents God's love and anger in vigorous and vivid language. Christ corrected many of the Old Testament's inadequate conceptions of God. In particular, Christ condemned the idea that we are to show vengeance on our enemies, or to take on ourselves the task of destroying those we consider to be the enemies of God. Parts of the Old Testament foreshadow Christ's teaching on love of enemies, though Christ went much further in teaching unlimited forgiveness. He is like the Old Testament when he reveals to us a God who cares passionately about his people. He had no hesitation in using examples of human love and indignation to make us see what God is like. 'If you then, who are evil, know how to give good gifts to your children, how much more will your Father in heaven give good things to those who ask him!' (Mt 7:11). The parable of the unmerciful servant (Mt 18:23-35) shows a king full of wrath against the servant to whom he had forgiven so much when that servant refused to pardon a fellow servant who owed him so little. No character in Christ's parables is meant to be an exact picture of God, yet this parable is clearly intended to show something in God corresponding to the just wrath of the king. Christ himself felt human emotions of grief and anger at the closed minds and hard hearts of those who rejected his message of love and distorted the truth of God. One Sabbath day Jesus entered a synagogue where a man present had a withered hand. Some of the worshippers were so totally lacking in pity for the man's misfortune that their only thought was to discredit Jesus as a bad Jew who would heal on the Sabbath. Jesus 'looked around at them with anger; he was grieved at their hardness of heart' (Mk 3:5). He also showed anger when he drove the money changers and traders out of the temple. They were cluttering up the court of the Gentiles with their tables of coins and pens of sacrificial animals, and frustrating one purpose of the temple which was to be 'a house of prayer for all the nations' (Mk 11:17).

God's Passionate Love

The Bible shows us a God who cares for his people with passionate love and is not indifferent to their behaviour but is saddened and angered by their wilful refusal to follow his ways. God's relationship with his people is a stormy one. He loves them tenderly, as a father and mother love their children and, also like human parents, he is sometimes exasperated by their wrong-headed fickleness and stubbornness. They in turn behave towards him in both childlike and childish ways. They approach him with fear and trembling, awestruck at the thought that he may be near them, yet at the same time yearning for his presence and for 'the light of his countenance' to shine upon them. They plead for his help and expostulate and complain bitterly when he appears to ignore them. Especially in the Old Testament we find God's people baring their hearts to him without reticence or inhibitions. The psalms are full of ardent longing, deep veneration and extravagant promises of devotion to God, yet also at times full of complaints about the way he treats his people. The prophets and kings also address God in this passionate way. The book of Job is probably the supreme example in the Old Testament of human protest to God against the injustice and unfairness of much human suffering.

Life in a human family in many ways reflects God's relationship with his people. The Bible often depicts God as the father and mother of his people who experiences something corresponding to the many emotions of human parents towards their children. 'As a father has compassion for his children, so the LORD has compassion for those who fear him' (Ps 103:13). Jeremiah heard God saying,

> Is Ephraim my dear son?
> Is he the child I delight in?
> As often as I speak against him,
> I still remember him.

> Therefore I am deeply moved for him;
> I will surely have mercy on him, says the LORD
> (Jer 31:20).

The thought of God as 'father' clearly has a key place in Christ's teaching. It begins the prayer he taught his followers and occurs in many of his sayings. He appears to have gone further than any Jewish teacher up till then in using the intimate term 'Abba', a child's word for his father, as his characteristic way of addressing God. Because the description of God as 'father' has the authority of Jesus it must always have a special place in Christian thought and devotion. Yet it is still an analogy and the limitations of human fathers must not be projected onto God. It is not the only way we can speak of God, and today we increasingly recognise that the Bible and Christ use terms drawn from mother love to bring out certain aspects of God's care. The prophet Isaiah wrote that God's love is more enduring and constant even than a mother's love for the child she bore (Isa 49:15). Christ used feminine imagery when he wept over Jerusalem and said, 'How often have I desired to gather your children together as a hen gathers her brood under her wings, and you were not willing!' (Lk 13:34).

The Biblical Basis of the Reproaches

The Bible's conception of a God who cares for his people in a deeply passionate way is clearly seen in the Good Friday Reproaches. They interpret the cross for us as the supreme instance of the lengths to which God will go because he loves us. There is no serene, aloof benevolence for the human race in the cross. Rather we see the suffering love of one in anguish for the plight of his children, a plight which humanity has brought on itself, though much human suffering is by innocent victims of the faults of others. The Reproaches show the good which God offers, the wilful choice of evil by humanity, and the pain of God in giving that lost good to the world.

The first part in the contrasts drawn in the Reproaches refers to some event in Israel's story as related in the Old Testament. Their structure is mainly based on a passage in Micah which represents God speaking to Israel in these words:

> 'O my people, what have I done to you?
> In what have I wearied you?

Answer me!
For I brought you up from the land of Egypt,
and redeemed you from the house of slavery;
and I sent before you Moses, Aaron, and Miriam ...' (Mic 6:3-4).

This is a fine example of the parallelism of Hebrew poetry where similar or contrasting things are brought together, sometimes in quite elaborate patterns. The Reproaches as a whole develop this parallelism with reiterated statements of what God has done for his people, contrasted with the details of Christ's passion. The main twofold contrast is between God's action and humanity's treatment of Christ, but there can also be parallels within each contrast, as:

For forty years I led you safely through the desert.
I fed you with manna from heaven,
and brought you to a land of plenty;
but you led your Saviour to the cross.

God's action is described by three examples of his care for the people and the contrast is with the single statement 'you led your Saviour to the cross'. In the next Reproach one statement tells of God's care and the people's response forms a triad:

I planted you as my fairest vine,
but you yielded only bitterness:
when I was thirsty you gave me vinegar to drink,
and you pierced your Saviour with a lance.

Even more important than their similar literary form, the Reproaches capture the spirit of the prophets by showing God in earnest debate with his people. In Micah chapter 6 God challenges the people to a court case, calling on the mountains to bear witness and judge (vv. 1-2). God reminds them of their rescue from Egypt and goes on to tell of his care for them in their desert wanderings 'that you may know the saving acts of the LORD' (v. 5). He continues by accusing them of crimes against the poor and the weak and threatens to punish them. Similar language of passionate debate is found in the reiterated chorus of the Reproaches:

My people, what have I done to you?
How have I offended you? Answer me!

It may seem strange that God should consider it necessary to argue with his people in this way and try to convince them of his justice. To a certain frame of mind it must seem seem undignified, the exact opposite of the attitude, 'Never explain, never apologise'. No doubt the devil in C. S. Lewis' *Screwtape Letters* would make a great point of God letting down the austere majesty of the spiritual realm by descending to passionate argument with humans. 'He's vulgar, Wormwood. He has a bourgeois mind' (*Screwtape* p 112). But the God who made the world and loves his human children has no need to stand on his dignity in dealing with them. The incarnation shows us a God who lays aside his dignity and fully identifies himself with the human race in its weakness and earth-bound state. The human aspects of God in the Old Testament are foreshadowings of the Word becoming flesh. Micah chapter 6 is similar to many other places where God gets into debate with his wayward children. Jeremiah heard God pleading with his people, 'What wrong did your ancestors find in me that they went far from me …' (Jer 2:5) and he goes on, like Micah, to list God's acts of blessing and the people's response:

> I brought you into a plentiful land
> to eat its fruits and good things.
> But when you entered you defiled my land,
> and made my heritage an abomination (v. 7).

The Tragic Element in Creation

The reason why God argues so vigorously with his people is his love and regard for them as beings whom he created free in order that they could love and obey him without being forced to do so. God cannot be indifferent to the fact that his people forsake him, who is the source of their life and happiness, and turn to what can only bring them misery. God takes responsibility for his creation while allowing it a certain amount of freedom. The universe depends completely on God for its existence at every moment of its history. Yet, in his gift of existence to the universe God voluntarily limited his power. 'In the act of creation, God makes room for something other than himself' (J. Polkinghorne, *Science and Creation* p 61). God made essentially dependent creatures, by creating them, to have a certain independence of himself just because they are other than him. 'God chose a world in which chance has a role to play, thereby both being responsible for the consequences accruing, and also accepting limitation of his power to control' (Polkinghorne p 63).

Creation, therefore, is no careless gesture which costs God nothing. It is an act of generous self-giving. It means that God accepts the consequences for something other than himself to which he has given space to be itself, with all that entails. God's love in creating involves the letting go of total control over what creation is. Otherwise the created universe would simply be an extension of God's self. God, the all-powerful, voluntarily limits his power by giving to what is other than himself 'the power of response', as W. H. Vanstone describes it (*Love's Endeavour, Love's Expense,* p 67). That is, God makes himself responsible for possible tragedy in the created world and redeems the tragedy by suffering love. Since the possible becomes actual in natural disaster and human wrongdoing, God's work of creation includes re-creation or redemption because God is infinite love and never abandons what he has made, no matter how far it has strayed from his ways. 'We may say that Christ, the Incarnate Word, discloses to us, at the climax of his life, what word it was that God spoke when"he commanded and they were created"' (Vanstone p 70).

The creation myths of many nations contain a similar insight when they make sacrifice an element of the story, more prominent in some than in others. These early myths do not expound the idea of creation out of nothing. They start with something already in existence – a cosmic egg, chaos or indeterminate matter – out of which the universe is formed. In the Hindu Rig Vedas creation occurs when the original man, Purusha, is dismembered and the parts of his body form the material world. Closely related to the idea of the primeval sacrifice is the thought of a cosmic battle by which the world is formed. Ancient Babylon has the story of the young god Marduk, who slew the monster Tiamat, dividing her body in two and making one part the earth and the other the sky which holds back the waters of chaos. The repeated sacrifices in many religions are meant to hold the universe in being against the forces that destroy it. In Egypt the daily offerings to the sun god were to ensure that each night would be followed by sunrise. Creation is seen not as a once-for-all event but a continual battle between creative forces and the powers of destruction.

The risk involved in creating a universe, the possibility of opposition to God's will and the anguishing responsibility that God accepts, are seen in their most extreme form in the case of human beings who can do so much harm to themselves and other creatures. Yet God, persumably, considered the risk worthwhile in order to allow the unforced response of love from his children. In giving us freedom God did not free himself from responsibility for the consequences we may suffer. He is like a parent who knows that children must be allowed some freedom to grow and mature, while always being available to them and sharing the consequences of their possible misuse of freedom. The parable of the prodigal son is a summary of human history in the form of a family story. The father in the story allowed his son the space to 'come to himself' (Lk 15:17) even though it meant that he squandered his inheritance and was reduced to eating pig's food. Throughout the son's painful journey to self-knowledge the father suffered with him, he was constantly on the lookout for his return and always ready to welcome him back. 'But while he was still far off, his father saw him and was filled with compassion; he ran and put his arms around him and kissed him' (Lk 15:20). The whole Bible is the story of the prodigal son writ large and tells us what is the cost to God of creating free human beings. The Bible picture of God is utterly different from the God of deism who, having created a universe, left it to itself.

God's responsibility for a world which he does not totally control may give some insight into the insoluble problem of suffering. Why does God allow people to die painfully in war, famine, earthquake and from incurable disease? Many have attempted to form a theodicy – a justification of God – by explaining how evils could occur in a world created by an all-loving, all-powerful being and thereby shift the blame for suffering away from God. But the Bible shows us a God who is ready to accept blame. The Old Testament depicts God not only as allowing suffering but also as its cause. 'Does disaster befall a city unless the LORD has done it?' (Am 3:6). No doubt the distinction between allowing and causing suffering is an important one, an advance on the Old Testament understanding which attributes everything directly to God. Yet we see in its way of speaking how much God bears responsibility for the world he has made. The passionate protests of the biblical writers are in keeping with God's responsibility for the state of the world and of human beings. We are right to protest against the seeming unfairness of innocent suffering, and even against the suffering of those not totally innocent, because it often seems out of proportion to the wrong they have done. Human wrongdoing falls within the sphere of God's responsibility. The Old Testament writers sometimes expressed this fact in a way unacceptable to our conviction of God's goodness. 'I [God] will harden his [Pharaoh's] heart, so that he will not let the people go' (Ex 4:21). The writer had such a strong sense of God's sovereignty over creation that he made God the cause of Pharaoh's cruelty. We cannot accept his words as they stand. It was a cruel king, not God, who treated the Hebrew slaves so harshly. Yet the biblical author showed that God, in making and sustaining a world with free human beings, makes himself responsible for the suffering which occurs. When God's people in their suffering cry out against their cruel fate, God hears their cries against himself. He does not leave others to take the blame.

We have already noted that the Old Testament writers complained vigorously to God about the pain they endured, uninhibited by any false reverence. The supreme example of the prayer of complaint is probably the book of Job. Job passionately protested his innocence before God and dared to demand of God why he should suffer as he does. 'See he will kill me; I have no hope; but I will defend my ways to his face. This will be my salvation, that the godless shall not come before him' (Job 13:15, 16). Job did not allow his three friends to get away with the conventional answer to his misfortunes, that somehow he must have deserved them. He accused them, 'Will you speak falsely for God, and speak deceitfully for him? Will you show partiality towards him, will you plead the case for God?' (Job 13:7, 8). Job maintained his integrity before God and dared to struggle with his suffering and with God. He complained bitterly that there is no impartial judge between God and human beings. How then can human complaints against God be heard?

> For he is not a mortal, as I am, that I might answer him,
> that we should come to trial together.
> There is no umpire between us,
> who might lay his hand on us both (Job 9:32, 33).

God's final answer to Job's protest is not found in the book of Job but in the coming of Christ. It is there that the responsibility of God for his creation receives its supreme expression. Christ, both God and man, is the 'umpire' between God and man whom Job demands. God became part of his own creation and shares its struggles. The cost to God of making a world containing free human beings was paid in full by God in Christ's crucifixion.

> This sacrifice is no after-thought invented to meet an unfortunate situation. Rather it belongs to the very constitution of the universe, to the very life of God himself. It was through sacrifice that the created world came into existence: it is through sacrifice that its evils are thwarted and overcome (F. W. Dillistone *The Christian Understanding of Atonement*, pp 249-50).

When Christ hung on the cross and cried out, 'My God, my God, why have you forsaken me?' God was joining in the anguished cry of the God-forsaken. Sydney Carter conveys this truth with tragic irony in his Good Friday hymn when he puts these words into the mouth of the robber on the cross:

> It's God they ought to crucify,
> Instead of you and me.
> I said to the carpenter
> A-hanging on the tree.

The Reproaches show us God sharing in the world's anguish. Their passionate language communicates something of the inner reality of the cross and may help us to know, in heart as well as head, the love of God which passes knowledge.

CHAPTER 2

The Exodus Theme

The *Via Dolorosa,* the way of the cross, has a special fascination for Christians as they think about the passion of Christ and try to grasp its meaning. The term describes both the physical journey to Calvary and also the whole passion considered as a journey whose destination was the world's redemption. The stations of the cross, beginning with Jesus sentenced to death and ending with his body being placed in the tomb, are a means of bringing home to us the depth of his love and the cost of our salvation, particularly if they are combined with a Good Friday procession. But the way of the cross can also be considered as a journey which Christ made from the glory of God's right hand to the degradation of death on a cross and the resulting exaltation by God, as it is described by St Paul in the familiar passage about the 'self-emptying' of Christ, which may be an early Christian hymn (Phil 2:6-11).

The journey of Christ to the cross and the journey of the Israelites from Egypt to the promised land are placed together in the Reproaches and contrasted with each other. Journeys lend themselves readily to symbolic treatment. Much of the world's great literature describes epic travel, and the movement from place to place through many dangers and against many obstacles becomes a metaphor to explore progress in understanding and spiritual achievement. The wanderings of Odysseus, from the plains of Troy to his home in Ithaca, awaken the reader to a knowledge of his own ideals and longings, strivings, failures and goals. Israel's desert wanderings provide Christians with the language to express God's work for human salvation – the journey from bondage under evil and all that dehumanises to freedom in fellowship with God and all redeemed creation. The parallel between the Israelites' journey to the promised land and Christ's journey to the cross is the basis of the Reproaches. Each of them refers either to the exodus journey as a whole, or particular events in it, and draws a contrast with Christ's passion or with some of its constituent parts. The Reproaches begin with the general statement 'I led you out of Egypt, from slavery to freedom' and go on to list the forty years' travel through the desert, the feeding with manna and provision of water from the rock, the crossing of the Red sea, the defeat of Israel's enemies and the settlement in the promised land. The last two Reproaches, 'I gave you a royal sceptre', 'I raised to the height of majesty', are probably best taken as stating the final result of God's deliverance of his people from bondage.

From Egypt to the Promised Land

The exodus journey is basic to an understanding of the Reproaches, so we shall outline its main features and discuss its significance both for Jews and Christians. The escape of the Israelites from Egypt, and their hazardous progress over forty years to the promised land, had a very important place in Jewish consciousness. Many of the Psalms celebrate the exodus (e.g. 78, 80, 105, 114); the prophets appeal to it in proclaiming God's plan and calling the people to faithfulness (e.g. Isa 63:11-13, Jer 31:32, Hos 11:1). The exodus is a journey of salvation, both in the material and spiritual senses. The Israelite slaves in Egypt were liberated from cruel bondage and hard labour and eventually reached a land where they governed themselves. Their journey was also one of discovery of themselves as God's covenant people who have the responsibility of obeying God's law.

It is a typically modern question to ask how much actual history, in the sense of provable fact, there is in the exodus story. That was not the concern of the biblical writers. They were concerned with seeing God's hand in a great act of deliverance. To use the story with integrity we must be convinced that it contains a basis of historic fact, since we cannot speak of God's action without referring to events that happened on this earth. But the emphasis of the Bible lies on God's purpose worked out in human history, not the details of the events themselves. This concern is even more important when we read the exodus story, as the early Christians did, as a foreshadowing of the mighty act of salvation achieved by Christ.

The saga of the exodus could be said to begin with the Passover on the night when Moses led the children of Israel out of Egypt in haste. A destroying angel slew the first born sons of the Egyptians, so that Pharaoh urged the Israelites to leave his land with their families, their cattle and all their possessions. They had eaten a hasty meal of unleavened bread and roast lamb. The blood of the lambs was sprinkled on their door posts as a sign to the destroying angel to 'pass over' their houses. But the Israelites were scarcely over the borders of Egypt when Pharaoh regretted his panic decision to give up a valuable source of slave labour. He set out with his armies in hot pursuit. The Israelites' joy at their escape quickly turned to dismay when they saw on the horizon the dust of Pharaoh's chariots. In their terror they turned to Moses with angry sarcasm, 'Was it because there were no graves in Egypt that you have taken us away to die in the wilderness?' (Ex 14:11). Moses calmed them down, assuring them, 'The LORD will fight for you, and you have only to keep still' (v. 14). He encouraged them to make an act of faith by walking over the dry sea bed, and when the pursuing Egyptians came there the returning waters engulfed them. God rescued his people from deadly peril and he continued to guide them on their long wanderings. The tradition expresses this guidance in vivid terms.

> The LORD went in front of them in a pillar of cloud by day, to lead them along the way, and in a pillar of fire by night, to give them light, so that they might travel by day and by night. Neither the pillar of cloud by day nor the pillar of fire by night left its place in front of the people (Ex 13:21, 22).

God's guidance and protection of his people did not exclude help by human agents. Moses relied on his brother-in-law, Hobab, for expert knowledge of the desert terrain. He said to him, 'Do not leave us, for you know where we should camp in the wilderness, and you will serve as eyes for us' (Num 10:31).

Attacks from hostile tribes were an ever-present danger to the migrating Israelites. When the Amalekites attacked them the battle swayed to and fro and the biblical author attributed the eventual victory of Israel to Moses holding up his hands, presumably in prayer to God (Ex 17:8-13). Sometimes they were defeated in battle (Num 14:45). Sometimes they asked for safe passage through other tribes' territory and on being refused they defeated the inhospitable people and occupied their land (Num 21:21-24). Balak, king of Moab, hoped to use the power of the prophet

Balaam's curse as an extra weapon in his armoury against Israel but God turned the curse into a blessing (Num 24:1-11).

When the Israelites came near the promised land they sent spies ahead to find out the strength of the native peoples. But on the spies' return, their nerve failed and they refused for a time to make the hazardous crossing of the river Jordan into a country whose inhabitants terrified them. In fact, they so discouraged the rest of the people that they were about to stone Moses and his faithful followers, Aaron, Joshua and Caleb, and return to Egypt. This aroused God's anger and he condemned the whole company to forty years' wandering and the cowardly spies to die by a plague (Num 14:26-35). Moses did not live to enter the promised land but he saw it from Mount Pisgah (Deut 34:1-6). His successor Joshua (whose name means 'Saviour' and is another form of the name 'Jesus') led the tribes over the Jordan and into many battles with the inhabitants before they finally settled in the land.

As well as facing human enemies on their journeys, the Israelites met the greater and more terrifying danger of death by hunger and thirst. When they had no food or water Egypt seemed very attractive to them. The horrors of slave labour were forgotten as they thought of 'the land of Egypt, when we sat by the fleshpots and ate our fill of bread' (Ex 16:3). In answer to their need and their grumbling, God sent them flesh in the form of quails, birds they could easily snare and cook, and 'manna' for bread. After a time they got fed up with the manna and craved the more exotic food of Egypt.

> If only we had meat to eat! We remember the fish we used to eat in Egypt for nothing, the cucumbers, the melons, the leeks, the onions, and the garlic; but now our strength is dried up, and there is nothing at all but this manna to look at. (Num 11:4-6).

Thirst, too, assailed them and God, through Moses, gave them water from a rock (Ex 17:1-7).

A key event in the biblical understanding of the exodus was the giving of the law to the people through Moses on Mount Sinai. When God rescued the Israelites from Egypt, he constituted them as his people through the covenant which he made with them and which was sealed by sacrifice. The covenant was not an agreement between equals but a gracious act of salvation by God, binding the people to himself and requiring from them obedience to his laws (Ex 24:1-11). But the people often proved unfaithful and disobedient. While Moses was on Mount Sinai, they persuaded Aaron to make them a golden calf which they worshipped with licentious rites (Ex 32:1-6). The calamities which befell the people on their wanderings were seen as God's punishment for their wrongdoing. But in spite of their grumbling, rebellion and sin, God never abandoned them. He disciplined and punished them and many of them died on their journeying but in the end he brought them to the land he had promised. The stormy relationship between God and his people through their long and eventful journey from Egypt to Israel is reflected in the language of the Reproaches, where God condemns, argues, pleads and speaks graciously to his pilgrim people today who have come into being through Christ's passion.

The feast of the Passover each year celebrates not just the escape from Egypt but the whole perilous journey to the promised land and God's continuing protection of his people. The Passover rite among Jews today includes a meal with many ceremonies recalling the events of the exodus and the recitation of God's acts in saving his people, usually in answer to ritual questions about the meaning of particular parts of the ceremonial. They recall the past events as a present reality because the God who brought their forbears out of Egypt is the saving God who upholds them in freedom.

> This promise, which has stood by our forefathers, stands by us; for it was not only one tyrant who planned our destruction; but in every generation men have sought to destroy us, and the Holy One, blessed be He, has delivered us from their hands…
>
> In each generation, every man is duty bound to envisage himself as though he personally took part in the Exodus from Egypt; as we read in the Torah: 'you shall tell your son on that day, saying "It is because of what the Lord did for me when I came forth from Egypt".' It was not only our forefathers that the Holy One, blessed be He, redeemed, He redeemed us, the living, together with them (*The Passover, the Last Supper and the Eucharist*, The Study Centre for Christian Jewish Relations, pp 10, 12).

Christ's 'Exodus'

The exodus theme is the basis of the Good Friday Reproaches. They contrast God's leading of his people from Egypt to the promised land with Christ's journey to the cross, and the first thing which strikes us is the great difference between the two. Yet this difference acquires greater force and significance because of the underlying similarity. The physical journey in both cases opens up a depth of meaning when it is seen as a mighty act of salvation by God. By bringing the two journeys together in this way, the Reproaches follow the New Testament in regarding Christ's life as the fulfilment of Israel's history. Christ in his own person sums up what God called Israel to be. God said to Jesus at his baptism, 'You are my Son, the Beloved; with you I am well pleased' (Mk 1:11), and Jeremiah heard God ask, 'Is Ephraim my dear son?' (Jer 31:20). St Matthew described the flight of the Holy Family to Egypt and their return as a fulfilment of Hosea's words, 'Out of Egypt I have called my son' (Mt 2:15. Hos 11:1). He understood Jesus as the fulfilment of Israel and his life as a new exodus. The prophets and psalms called Israel God's vine or vineyard (Isa 5:1,2. Jer 2:21. Ps 80:8-19) which often failed to produce good fruit. Christ is the true vine (Jn 15:1-11). In a different metaphor, he is the son of the vineyard's owner whom the tenant farmers kill and throw out of the vineyard when he comes for the fruit which they owe (Mk 12:1-12).

The New Testament writers and Christ himself often used the language of the Old Testament to describe Christ's ministry. In particular, the Passover ritual gave them terms and concepts by which to speak of his passion. Christ was crucified at Passover time and the celebration of the exodus enabled the early Christians to see Christ's death and resurrection as a new exodus to be celebrated by a new Passover. Christ connected the two when he said, 'I have eagerly desired to eat this Passover with you before I suffer' (Lk 22:15). In the first three gospels the last supper was a Passover meal. St John, on the other hand, represented the crucifixion as taking place on the day of preparation for the Passover (19:31) but even more than the other evangelists he used Passover themes to bring out the meaning of the passion. Near the beginning of the gospel, John the Baptist described Jesus as 'the lamb of God' (Jn 1:35). In St John's passion narrative Jesus hung on the cross through the afternoon of 'the day of Preparation for the Passover' which was the time when the passover lambs were being killed (Jn 19:14,31). According to John the two robbers who were crucified with Jesus had their legs broken to hasten death but, since Jesus was dead already, he escaped this indignity 'so that the scripture might be fulfilled, "None of his bones shall be broken"' (19:36). There is clearly an allusion here to the Passover lamb, regarding which the law decreed 'you shall not break any of its bones' (Ex 12:46). St Paul wrote, 'For our paschal lamb, Christ, has been sacrificed' (1 Cor 5:7). In St Luke's account of the transfiguration, when Moses and Elijah appeared with Jesus they 'were speaking of his departure (Greek, *exodos*), which he was about to accomplish at Jerusalem' (Lk 9:31).

The early church continued to use Passover language to celebrate Christ's redemption. They took over the word Passover in its Greek form *Pascha* as the name for the festival of Christ's death and resurrection, considered as one great act of God. Many languages (e.g. the French *Pâques* and the Irish *Cáisc*) use forms of the Greek word to indicate the festival which in English is called Easter. Today we think of Good Friday as the commemoration of Christ's death and Easter Sunday the festival of his resurrection, but the original unity of the two is seen in the Easter Vigil service where the drama of the salvation Christ won for us is proclaimed using Passover terminology.

> For this is the Passover of that true Lamb of God,
> by whose blood the homes of all the faithful
> are hallowed and protected (*Lent Holy Week Easter*, p 231).

In comparing the exodus journey with Christ's passion, it is helpful to compare Moses with Christ. The New Testament writers find some resemblance between the two as agents of God's deliverance, in the one case from Egyptian slavery and in the other from sin and separation from God. The baby Moses was in danger of being killed along with all the Israelite boys at the king of Egypt's orders. St Matthew told how King Herod ordered all the male babies in Judea to be slaughtered. Moses obeyed God at the cost of his own comfort and safety, first when he left Pharaoh's court and saw the suffering of his own people, and then when he gave up life as a shepherd in the land of Midian and returned to Egypt to oppose a mighty king. Christ, as St Paul said, 'though he was in the form of God ... emptied himself, taking the form of a slave ... and became obedient to the point of death – even death on a cross' (Phil 2:6-8). Moses had to face the anger and rejection of the Israelite people on several occasions, as when they were frightened by Pharaoh's pursuing armies and by fears of death through hunger and thirst. Jesus was a prophet without honour in his own country and rejected by the Passover crowd in favour of the brigand Barabbas. The Jews credited Moses with the gift of manna to feed the people when they were starving in the desert. When Jesus fed the five thousand the people hailed him as a new Moses, 'the prophet who is to come into the world' (Jn 6:14, alluding to Deut 18:15). Moses shared the dangers and hardships of the escape from Egypt. Jesus' life, death and resurrection was the pioneer journey by which all who believe in him are led from the exile of separation from God to new life in his presence.

Yet the differences between Moses and Christ are much more striking. Moses led the people out of bondage as a free man. The New Testament writers described Christ as the paschal lamb by whose death the people were freed. If Moses had been killed by Pharaoh, or kept as a slave in Egypt as the price of the people's freedom, that would have been a closer parallel to the salvation Christ brought to the world. Moses had a minor role in the manna which God sent to feed the people. Like them, he satisfied his own hunger by eating the manna. Christ, by contrast, is himself the bread of life which feeds a hungry world and in order to become that bread he had first to give up his life in death. When Moses obeyed God's call he faced danger and difficulty. Christ's act of obedience was a complete self-emptying which culminated in an agonising and shameful death on a cross. Christ is the saviour of the world. We cannot say in that direct and radical sense that Moses is the saviour of the Jewish people. God is their saviour and Moses had an important role as God's servant in their rescue from Egypt. But Jesus is more than God's servant; God fully and uniquely identified himself with Jesus in the salvation of the world.

Just as there is this great contrast between Moses and Jesus superimposed on an underlying similarity, so the Reproaches bring out the nature of Christ's salvation by highlighting the contrast between the fate of Jesus and God's rescue of the children of Israel. To redeem a fallen race Christ did in reverse what God had done for Israel. The journey Christ made is the opposite to that of God's people from Egyptian slavery to freedom in the promised land. Christ's journey began in the courts of heaven, from where he came down to this earth and lived a truly human life which culminated in his being made a prisoner and expelled from the chosen people. He was handed over to foreigners, made to walk out of the holy city, stripped of his clothes, and nailed to a cross where he cried, 'My God, my God, why have you forsaken me?' (Mk 15:34). The details of Christ's fate, in contrast to the Israelites' journey, are used by the Reproaches to show us more clearly the cost of our salvation and to appreciate its wonder.

Underlying the explicit contrast of the Reproaches is the basic comparison between the eternal nature of Christ and his fate at the hands of those who crucified him. In the developed thought of the New Testament, Christ is seen as one and coeternal with God (Jn 1:1,2) and as God's agent in the creation and preservation of the universe (Jn 1:3; Col 1:15-17). Yet he lived on earth in human weakness, without any privileges of wealth or class, and was arrested, bound, mocked, led from one court to another, condemned, flogged, led through jeering crowds to gallow's hill where he was executed in the cruel Roman manner with that day's batch of criminals. Christians came to see that only he whose nature was divine could make a sufficient sacrifice to save us and that our salvation needed the sinless one to identify himself with us in our separation from God, bearing the penalty of human sin.

Sharing in Christ's Exodus

Christ's passion is the fulfilment of the exodus. The experience of Christ on earth paralleled the exodus journey, with the important contrasts which we noted but with an underlying similarity. The result of Christ's passion, the redeemed and forgiven people of God, was also described in exodus terms by the early Christians. Christ was the pioneer on a journey in which he invites all people to share. St Paul retold the exodus story as an experience both of Israel and of the Christian Church (1 Cor 10:1-11). He described the Israelites' passage through the Red sea as 'baptism' (v. 2) and understood that they were in some sense redeemed by Christ, 'For they drank from the spiritual rock that followed them, and the rock was Christ' (v. 4). He claimed that the events of the exodus 'were written down to instruct us, on whom the ends of the ages have come' (v. 11). He used the faults of the Israelites on their journey from Egypt to the promised land as a warning to the Corinthian Christians not to repeat their sins, so he must have have thought of the Christian Church as also undergoing an exodus deliverance.

The early Christians developed the idea that the journey of the Israelites prefigured the salvation which they had found in Christ. They thought of themselves, before they knew Christ, as like the Israelite slaves in Egypt and the release which Christ brought them as their exodus. Baptism, the sacrament of their salvation, was often portrayed as a crossing of the Red Sea and in parts of the early church the rite of baptism included the giving of milk and honey to the new Christians as a symbol of their entry to the promised land of fellowship with God. The normal time for baptism was at Easter, the Christian passover, and the associations of the original passover contributed greatly to the language of Easter praise, as in the hymn of St John of Damascus:

Come, ye faithful, raise the strain
Of triumphant gladness:
God has brought his Israel
Into joy from sadness;
Loosed from Pharaoh's bitter yoke
Jacob's sons and daughters;
Led them with unmoistened foot
Through the Red Sea waters (Tr John M. Neale).

Victims in the Exodus Story

There is one remaining matter to be dealt with when we think of the exodus theme in relation to Christ's journey to the cross. A part of God's care and protection of Israel, according to the Reproaches, is his destruction of Israel's enemies. 'For your sake I scourged your captors and first born sons, but you brought your scourges down on me.' 'I ... drowned your captors in the sea but you handed me over to your high priests.' 'For you I struck down the kings of Canaan, but you struck my head with a reed.' Should we exult over the defeat of our enemies in this way? Several modern versions of the Reproaches (such as the English Joint Liturgical Group's *Holy Week Services* 1971, 1983, the Church of England *Lent, Holy Week and Easter* 1984 and the Canadian *Book of Alternative Services* 1985) leave out these references to the destruction of Israel's enemies.

The traditional Reproaches quite unselfconsciously use the Old Testament language of God protecting his people and, in consequence, destroying the enemies who often oppressed them cruelly. There is no stress on the destruction of Israel's enemies; that is incidental to the salvation of God's people. Yet the question must arise sooner or later about the suffering of others which is involved in the rescue of the chosen people and in their finding a land of their own. This is recognised in the Jewish Passover ritual. A drop of wine is spilled at the mention of the ten plagues in Egypt 'as a symbol of regret that the victory had to be purchased through misfortune visited upon God's creation, the Egyptians' (*The Passover, the Last Supper and the Eucharist*, p 11).

But the most significant fact in the Christian use of Old Testament language in the Reproaches about the overthrow of Israel's enemies is that Christ himself suffered a similar fate. If the salvation of God's people required suffering, then Christ shared in that suffering to the full. God redeemed humanity not by destroying human beings but by submitting in Christ to the sorrow and pain people impose on each other. The contrast drawn in the Reproaches between God's care of his people and their treatment of Jesus becomes all the more heightened when we note that Christ himself was scourged, that God gave up his first-born, his only Son, to the death of the cross. The first-born sons of the Egyptians died at the exodus of the Israelites from Egypt. It was God's only Son who died at the exodus which was the redemption of the world. Christ's cross was a baptism, a cup of suffering (Mk 10:38) more severe than drowning in the Red Sea. It is understandable that modern people should feel uncomfortable with references to God's destruction of enemies, and the structure of the Reproaches lends itself to variety of content when such references can be left out. Yet there is value in remembering the total history of the chosen people, including its tragic and cruel episodes. The salient fact is that Christ himself submitted to the pain and suffering visited on the enemies of God's people. The sinless one bore the penalty of sinners and in that fact lies our redemption. We can find in the Christian gospel the strength to face up to the horrors of human history because Christ's cross declares to us a God who takes responsibility for his creation to the extent that he fully shares its suffering and redeems the tragedy with the outpouring of new life.

CHAPTER 3

Christ Led to the Cross

God led his ancient people Israel from slavery in Egypt to freedom in a land flowing with milk and honey, and he leads the human race from bondage under dehumanising evil to freedom and fullness of life in fellowship with himself and renewed creation. Israel's migration is a parable of the human journey to full humanity, which is only possible through Christ's journey to the cross. We human beings led Jesus Christ to a cross, and that event, both a horrible crime and also a glorious act of salvation, gives us the power to be truly human as God meant us to be. The Good Friday Reproaches use Israel's exodus journey as the basis for contemplating Christ's journey to the cross. They contrast God's gentle leading of his people and care for their welfare with the cruel behaviour of Jesus' captors who led him with blows and insults to the degradation and agony of crucifixion. We can best understand the Reproaches as a contrast between the human journey on which God leads all of us and the journey to the cross which all human sin inflicted on God's Son. Christ's journey to the cross makes our journey to true humanity possible.

The contrast between the two journeys, as presented in the Reproaches, is striking.

> I led you out of Egypt, from slavery to freedom,
> but you led your Saviour to the Cross ...
> I planted you as my fairest vine,
> but you yielded only bitterness ...
> I opened the sea before you,
> but you opened my side with a spear ...
> I raised you to the height of majesty,
> but you raised me high on a cross.

The poignancy of the words is further heightened when the first person singular is used both in statement and counter statement:

'*I* led you ..., but you led *me* ...' God, the creator and redeemer of the world, identified himself fully with his Son Jesus Christ who was crucified. The redeemer became a captive and only by submitting to captivity could he redeem. The chief priests and hostile crowd taunted Jesus on the cross, 'He saved others; he cannot save himself' (Mk 15:29-32), stating with unconscious irony the profound truth that Christ, precisely through his powerlessness, suffering and subjection to the forces of evil, released humanity from their bondage.

Christ Handed Over

Each of the Reproaches depicts Christ as the object of some hostile action, whether it is mockery, contempt or torture. Recurring phrases like 'You led me ...,' 'You handed me over ...,' indicate how Jesus allowed himself to be subjected to the will of cruel men throughout his passion. The word 'to hand over', *paradidonai*, occurs throughout the passion narratives and Raymond Brown notes (*The Death of the Messiah,* p 211) that it was a technical legal term for consigning criminals to judges and executioners and that it is also used in the New Testament to state that God 'did not withhold his own Son, but gave him up (*paradóken*) for all of us' (Rom 8:32). The phrase 'did not withhold' echoes the story of Abraham and his son Isaac where Abraham was ready to sacrifice Isaac at God's command but at the last moment God told him to spare him. '[God] said, "Do not lay your hand on the boy or do anything to him; for now I know that you fear God, since you have not withheld your son, your only son, from me"' (Gen 22:12).

What God did not demand of Abraham, he required of himself for the salvation of the world. It is significant that the same word is used for God's purpose as for the evil actions of Judas, the Sanhedrin, the Passover crowds and Pilate. God does not take away human freedom but incorporates even its misuse in the divine plan of salvation, which was only possible at the cost of Christ's suffering. The first three gospels emphasise how Jesus was the victim of the world's malice. 'The Son of Man is betrayed into the hands of sinners' (Mk 14:41). 'They crucified Jesus there with the criminals' (Lk 23:33). The concern of John's gospel, on the other hand, was to show that Jesus was totally at one with his Father in his being given up to death for our salvation.

'For this reason the Father loves me, because I lay down my life in order to take it up again. No one takes it from me, but I lay it down of my own accord. I have power to lay it down, and I have power to take it up again. I have received this command from my Father' (Jn 10:17, 18). As God's victorious Son and the agent of God's mighty act of redemption, Jesus was in control of events throughout. St Paul also understood Christ as active in his sufferings, describing him as the one 'who loved me and gave (*paradontos*) himself for me' (Gal 2:20). This inner, eternal truth of the passion in no way denies the brutal fact that the authorities of the time put to death an innocent man who was without worldly power. Jesus freely, in obedience to his Father's will, submitted to human malice, injustice and cruelty in order to redeem a sinful human race. St Luke described the action of Pilate as 'He handed Jesus over as they wished (literally, 'to their will')' (*ton de Iesoun paredóken tó thelémati autón*) (Lk 23:25). His words could apply to the whole series of events from Christ's arrest in the garden of Gethsemane to his death on the cross. All that time Jesus was totally under the control of others. Judas betrayed (*paredóken*) him to the soldiers in the garden. They led him bound to trial before the supreme Jewish council, the Sanhedrin, who in turn handed him over to the Roman governor, Pontius Pilate. He suffered rough horse play from both the Jewish and the Roman soldiers. According to Luke, Pilate sent him to Herod, the Jewish ruler of Galilee, who sent him back to Pilate. The Jerusalem crowds yelled 'Crucify him!' He suffered the ordeal of scourging. Pilate condemned him to death and consigned him to his soldiers for execution. The soldiers led, or more likely drove, him with two other felons through the public streets to the place of execution on the main thoroughfare outside the city walls. The cruel, degrading procession to Calvary, with the centurion shouting 'Whip the prisoners forward!', well portrays the journey which Christ made for our salvation. The words of the risen Christ to Peter, 'But when you grow old, you will stretch out your hands, and someone else will fasten a belt around you and take you where you do not wish to go' (Jn 21:18), were a poignant reflection of Christ's own death. At the cross Jesus was stripped of his clothes and nailed to the wooden beams where he hung unable to move any part of his body but his head. It is a picture of utter subjection to human cruelty and injustice. Yet in this very fact Christ achieved the defeat of evil and demonstrated the power of love. We see in the journey of the cross, and in the episodes which it contains, the work of God making possible the human journey to wholeness and new life. Details of its episodes help us to see different facets of God's victory over evil through Christ.

Jesus and the Sanhedrin

After Jesus was betrayed and arrested in the garden he was brought from one courtroom to another for his different trials. The Reproaches state: 'you handed me over to your high priests', 'you led me to Pilate's court', indicating both the Jewish and the Roman elements in the condemnation of Christ. Why was Jesus put to death? The Christian faith sees the crucifixion as the outworking of God's purpose for the world's salvation. 'Christ died for our sins in accordance with the scriptures' (1 Cor 15:3). But God's purpose was realised on this earth through the interaction of human beings with their various political, social and religious aims. It is useful to look at the mundane reasons for the death of Christ because they throw light on God's working to redeem human beings from the sins which brought Jesus to the cross. The Reproaches refer to different events in Christ's passion to show how sinful humanity treated its saviour and how God brought salvation out of these wicked actions.

The chief priests, as leaders of the Sanhedrin, were the opponents of Jesus most intent on his death. But we need to look at the broader picture to see how his whole public ministry roused the opposition of the religious leaders of his time and nation. Almost from the start, Jesus found himself at odds with the Pharisees, the strict Jews who prided themselves on their meticulous observance of the law of Moses as it was elaborated by the scribes into a long code of rules. They were genuinely offended by what appeared to them the lax behaviour of Jesus and his disciples regarding the law. Some of Christ's severest words were against the Pharisees, though a few like Nicodemus were attracted by his teaching. Yet it was the Saducees, the worldly, wealthy Jewish priests who masterminded and set in motion the plans to capture Jesus and condemn him to death. Supported by Pharisees, scribes and elders they determined to have Jesus killed even before his last journey to Jerusalem, according to John's gospel (Jn 11:45-53). Why were they so opposed to him? Jesus was a prophet and prophets are uncomfortable people to any community and often have to pay a severe price for their hard words. In addition, Jesus went further than any of the prophets in the claims he made for his special relationship with God and his cavalier attitude to established traditions and ideas. His association with the dregs of society and with the hated tax collectors who worked for the oppressive Roman regime was an offence to many. A good number of people were drawn to Jesus by the attraction of his sheer love and goodness and by the unique authority which he showed, but others were deeply disturbed by his presence and sometimes begged him to go away and leave them alone, like the Gerasenes when he healed a demoniac near their town (Mk 5:17). In fact, Christ's life and fate were foreshadowed in the picture of the righteous man in the book of Wisdom who aroused the envy of those around him:

> He became to us a reproof of our thoughts;
> the very sight of him is a burden to us,
> because his manner of life is unlike that of others,
> and his ways are strange...
> Let us condemn him to a shameful death,
> for, according to what he says, he will be protected
> (Wis 2:14-15,20).

The temple in Jerusalem had a key role in the condemnation of Jesus by the Sanhedrin. One of the charges against him at his trial was that he had threatened to destroy the temple 'made with hands' and in three days build another 'not made with hands' (Mk 14:58). In the light of Christ's resurrection, John saw a profound meaning in those words, that they referred to Christ's crucified and risen body (Jn 2:21-22), but they were seen by the Jewish leaders as a challenge to the whole temple system and were connected with Christ's cleansing of the temple which John placed at the beginning of his ministry. The other gospels set this event in the last week of Christ's life and Mark represented it as the final act which led to his arrest and condemnation (Mk 11:18). Jesus was acting in the spirit of the prophets when he drove the money changers and the dealers in sacrificial animals out of the temple. He quoted words of Isaiah and Jeremiah, 'Is it not written, "My house shall be called a house of prayer for all nations"? But you have made it a den of robbers' (Mk 11:17, Isa 56:7, Jer.7:11). Jeremiah brought on himself the wrath of the priests and prophets of his day and was almost killed when he said that, because of the people's wickedness, the city with its temple would be destroyed (Jer 26).

The members of the Sanhedrin, like their predecessors, probably thought they had good reason to destroy Jesus. His cleansing of the temple was a direct challenge to the authority and the livelihood of the chief priests who were the appointed guardians of the temple worship. Many of the Sanhedrin were genuinely offended by his apparent flouting of the Sabbath laws. His criticism of the multitude of rules, by which the scribes sought to make the law of Moses applicable to every conceivable situation, would have seemed to them an attack on true religion. The more politically minded of the Sanhedrin, the chief priests, probably felt that Jesus was a danger to the Jewish state. They feared that his growing popularity with the masses would incite a revolt against Roman rule. Being political realists they knew that a rebellion was bound to fail and likely to result in the suppression of the Jewish state by the Romans, as indeed happened after the Zealots' revolt in A.D. 66-70. Hence they had good 'reasons of state' for the elimination of Jesus. People are often most cruel to others when they are fearful, under threat and uncertain of their future. The instinct for self preservation drowns the voice of conscience. What is the life of one person compared with the welfare of the entire population? Caiaphas, the high priest, put the matter plainly to the council: 'It is better for you to have one man die for the people than to have the whole nation destroyed' (Jn 11:50). This is one of the many instances of dramatic irony in the gospels. The words of Caiaphas were true in a sense he never dreamed of, as St John commented, 'He did not say this on his own, but being high priest that year he prophesied that Jesus was about to die for the nation, and not for the nation only, but to gather into one the dispersed children of God' (vv. 51-52).

The condemnation of Jesus by the chief priests and other members of the Sanhedrin was due to a mixture of self-seeking, malice, jealousy, fear, cruelty and political intrigue, very ordinary sins found in every age and society. We regard their action as the most appalling crime to stain the pages of history because of our estimate of the character and divine nature of our Lord, but the most appalling thing about it is that it was done by relatively ordinary people and not by the world's greatest sinners. There was an element, too, of sincere religious conviction on the part of at least some of the Sanhedrin in their opposition to Christ. Brown states, 'The Gospel portrait implies that Jesus would be found guilty by the self-conscious religious majority of any age and background' (*The Death of the Messiah*, p 393). Typical, unexceptional, human sins brought Jesus to the cross. They were laid on him, the sinless victim. He broke their power and made possible our release from their dominion.

Jesus and Pontius Pilate

> I led you on your way in a pillar of cloud,
> but you led me to Pilate's court.

The Sanhedrin condemned Jesus to death but he was actually sentenced and executed by the Roman administration in Judea. It is a complex question how far the rights of the Jewish authorities extended under Roman rule and, in particular, whether or not they could inflict the death penalty. When Jesus was faced with the woman taken in adultery her accusers clearly thought they had the right to stone her to death (Jn 8:3-11), a punishment they actually carried out on Stephen, the first Christian martyr (Acts 7:58-60). Yet Paul was rescued by the Roman tribune when he was in danger of being killed in Jerusalem (Acts 23:12-15). It seems that the situation varied with the gravity of the accusation and with the firmness of the Roman rulers at various times. Probably the Romans would have tolerated stoning by Jews for purely religious offences committed by their own people but, if an alleged crime had any political implications, a conscientious governor would feel bound to take notice. Jewish disputes about the Messiah could have affected the security of the state and the chief priests cleverly represented Jesus as a threat to Roman rule. They may also have wished to transfer some of the responsibility for Jesus' death on to the hated occupying power. Though they had successfully manipulated the Jerusalem mob to shout for Jesus to be crucified, they knew that he was very popular in the country at large and they wanted him condemned and executed without provoking a public outcry. It was in their interest to involve the Roman government of the time in the death of Jesus. Christ was the victim of a complex mixture of political and religious intrigue. He allowed himself to be caught up in the cross currents of the human and social networks to which we cannot help belonging and which are marked by all the defects of our fallen nature. The system claimed him as its victim and, through his patient endurance of suffering and love for his persecutors, he redeemed the world from evil.

Pontius Pilate, prefect of Judea and Samaria in the time of Christ, has become more famous than many kings and leaders of much higher position and greater importance than he. Only three human beings are mentioned by name in the Apostles' and Nicene Creeds, our Lord Jesus Christ, the Blessed Virgin Mary and Pontius Pilate. He is not to be envied for his fame since it reminds the world of his share in the death of Christ. All the gospels portray him as unwilling to condemn Jesus. He found himself in a difficult situation and reacted to it in a way which was to earn him unwanted fame for countless generations to come. A man of equestrian rank, that is of the lesser nobility in Rome, he came to Judea in the pride of imperial power and contempt for the subject people he ruled. He was tactless and insensitive to Jewish feeling. He had his soldiers carry images of the Emperor into Jerusalem and enraged the Jews who considered that the holy city was contaminated by idolatry. A number of them came to him at his headquarters in Caesarea to protest against the images. Pilate at first refused to remove the imperial emblems and threatened to have his soldiers kill the protesters if they persisted in their demands, but when they showed themselves ready to die for their convictions he gave in to them and removed the offending objects from Jerusalem. On another occasion he was blamed for the death of some Galileans in connection with religious rites. 'At that very time there were some present who told him about the Galileans whose blood Pilate had mingled with their sacrifices' (Lk 13:1). The details of this episode are unknown but it obviously made him a hated figure.

Yet Pilate tried to be a conscientious government official and to administer impartial Roman justice, as his conduct at Christ's trial shows. In his judgement, Jesus was not guilty of any crime against the Roman administration. If, as Caiaphas and the Sanhedrin thought, the activity of Jesus might heighten Jewish national consciousness to the point of rebellion, that was not a just cause to condemn Jesus himself as a rebel against Rome. But the chief priests had cleverly won over the Jerusalem crowds to demand the death of Jesus and they accused Pilate of disloyalty to Caesar if he acquitted him. Pilate saw that to act with strict justice was politically and personally inexpedient. A Jerusalem mob at Passover time was a volatile and frightening thing for any Roman governor. In view of his past unfortunate handling of Jewish crises, Pilate would naturally be averse to taking political risks. No doubt he could have quelled a riot with the Roman garrison but the disturbance might have escalated to a fullscale revolt and, in any case, it would have been hard to explain to his superior officers in Syria and Rome that he had provoked all that trouble and possible bloodshed merely to save the life of a Jew. So he gave in to the demands of the chief priests and the crowds whom they had incited to have Jesus condemned to the cross.

The members of the Sanhedrin were more hostile to Jesus than Pilate was, the religious authority more ready to persecute than the secular one. It was so in the case of the prophet Jeremiah as well. His most bitter opponents were the religious leaders of his day. 'Then the priests and the prophets said to the officials and to all the people, "This man deserves the sentence of death because he has prophesied against this city, as you have heard with your ears"' (Jer 26:11). Jeremiah defended his conduct before the combined body of civil and religious powers (not so clearly distinguished then as they are now), with the result that 'the officials and all the people said to the priests and the prophets, "This man does not deserve the sentence of death, for he has spoken to us in the name of the LORD our God"' (v. 16). The state officials were not always so considerate to him and King Jehoiakim would have imprisoned and probably executed him if he had had the chance (Jer 36:26), but at least once Jeremiah was saved from the jealousy of priests and prophets by the intervention of the civil power.

It is interesting to compare Pilate's conduct in his trial of Jesus with that of other Roman governors faced with similar problems. A Roman tribune rescued Paul from being lynched by a Jerusalem crowd and sent him under heavy guard to the governor, Felix, in Caesarea (Acts 21:31; 23:23-24). Felix was more wily than Pilate and managed to avoid condemning Paul without antagonising the Jews. He simply did nothing beyond keeping Paul in prison until his term of office expired and he left the problem to Festus, his successor. Festus was a more straightforward man and gave Paul a proper trial, but even he tried hard to keep on the right side of his subjects (Acts 25:9) and was probably relieved when Paul appealed to the emperor and took the case out of his hands. Both these governors had a less difficult situation than Pilate because there could have been no pretext that Paul was a threat to Roman rule.

Another remarkable case of a man accused by the Jews and tried by the Romans concerns a namesake of our Lord. Jesus, son of Ananus, came into Jerusalem four years before the ill-fated rebellion against the Romans broke out and prophesied that the city and its temple would be destroyed. The leading Jews were naturally offended by his words, gave him a severe beating and ordered him to stop, but he persisted. They hauled him before the Roman procurator, Albinus, who had him 'whipped till his bones were laid bare' (Josephus) but he would not cease his dire warnings. Albinus concluded that he was a madman and let him go free. He continued to cry out, 'Woe, woe to Jerusalem', up to the beginning of the war and throughout the period of the siege until the city was finally sacked.

Pilate's vacillating conduct and his attempts to be conscientious foiled by political ambition and desire for self-preservation were among the causes of Christ's death. Jesus bore the burden of sin which is a mixture of weakness, good intentions, the desire to shift responsibility, the natural wish to save one's own skin and the reluctant agreement to collude with evil in the hope that good may come. By suffering these very prevalent features of human sin Christ offers us forgiveness and the moral strength to do right.

The Sanhedrin and the Roman governor had Jesus put to death because they wished to prevent unpleasant consequences for themselves and the Jewish state. But the very things they wished to avoid later happened. The chief priests feared that Jesus would be the occasion of a revolt against Roman rule, which would be ruthlessly suppressed and the nation destroyed. Less than thirty years later, the Zealot party among the Jews incited a country wide revolt and the Roman legions sacked Jerusalem and brought the Jewish nation to an end. Long before that, Pilate's rule had ended in disgrace. He was governor of Samaria as well as Judea and he was even less successful in his dealings with the Samaritans. A Samaritan prophet had claimed that he would show the sacred vessels of Moses on Mount Gerizim. Crowds of people were gathering to the site and Pilate, fearing a revolt, ordered his soldiers to block access to the mountain. There was a riot, some people were killed and the leaders were executed. The Samaritans complained to Pilate's superior, Vitellius the governor of Syria, who sent Pilate back to Rome to answer for his conduct. Often the good we do evil to achieve never comes, and the evil we try to prevent by evil means happens anyway. Christ redeems us from our incompetence along with our sins.

Jesus and the People

We have noted in passing the place of ordinary people, the populace at large, in the condemnation of Jesus. Their most prominent role was in the trial before Pilate when they shouted 'Crucify him!' The Reproaches state, 'You led your Saviour to the cross … You handed me over to your high priests … You led me to Pilate's court'. The only acceptable reference for the word 'you' is to the whole human race, and that is quite clearly how the Reproaches understand it since the congregation responds, 'Holy is God … have mercy on us.' As a matter of historical fact the chief priests themselves sent a squad of soldiers to arrest Jesus and, according to the gospels, they did so by stealth because they feared his popularity with the ordinary people would make a public arrest and trial difficult. Yet the people had a place in the death of Jesus. We have emphasised the representative character of those responsible for our Lord's crucifixion. The members of the Sanhedrin and the Roman governor were not the world's greatest sinners but showed the characteristics of people in every age and country. The citizens of Jerusalem and the Passover visitors to the city at the time of Christ's death showed the usual human mixture found in any large groups. Many of them were enthusiastic, generous and easily moved to pity, anger or hate. In the gospel records of the passion, the crowds showed many moods. They waved palm branches and cried 'Hosanna!' when Jesus rode into Jerusalem on a donkey and they continued to praise him in the temple courts. During the trial before Pilate, a crowd incited by Sanhedrin members demanded that the brigand Barabbas be released and Jesus crucified. On the way to the place of execution, according to Luke's passion narrative, 'A great number of the people followed him, and among them were women who were beating their breasts and wailing for him' (Lk 23:27). At the cross the chief priests, scribes and many bystanders took sadistic pleasure in jeering at

Christ and taunting him for his miserable fate. 'Those who passed by derided him, shaking their heads and saying, "Aha! You who would destroy the temple and build it in three days, save yourself, and come down from the cross!"' (Mk 15:29-30). Yet, again according to Luke, many also were sympathetic. 'And when all the crowds who had gathered there for this spectacle saw what had taken place, they returned home, beating their breasts. But all his acquaintances, including the women who had followed him from Galilee, stood at a distance, watching these things' (Lk 23:48-49).

Jerusalem was a large city for that time and during the Passover its population would have been swollen by pilgrims. Hence when 'the people' or 'the crowds' are mentioned it is not necessarily the same group which is referred to, though there was probably some overlap between the different groups. We have no grounds for claiming that exactly the same people who shouted 'Hosanna!' on Palm Sunday yelled 'Crucify him!' on Good Friday. Yet crowds are easily swayed. Caught up in the enthusiasm of the moment many people would cheer with the rest in the presence of a popular leader and equally succumb to agitators who could incite them to favour one prisoner while rejecting another with scorn. Included among the sins which brought Jesus to the cross were the volatile, unreliable emotions of all of us, especially in our susceptibility to peer pressure, group influence, party spirit or the domination of faction, cause or demagogue. Jesus bore the suffering which comes from our weakness in the face of those who manipulate us and, through his passion, strengthens us to repent and stand up against the malign influence of hatred, prejudice and mob rule.

The journey to the cross which Jesus undertook was a mission of rescue for a captive human race. The irony is that those who crucified him, representative of all of us, were the captives he came to save. They inflicted this journey on Jesus, but at the level of God's purpose he went to the cross in willing obedience to the Father whose love for sinful humanity he fully shared. 'You led your Saviour to the cross', and because he accepted this fate he truly became our Saviour.

CHAPTER 4

Christ Mocked and Scourged

Jesus Insulted

Death by crucifixion was not only extremely painful, it was also deeply humiliating. The Romans used this form of execution only for slaves and foreigners, never for Roman citizens. Hence the word 'crucified' implied the utmost contempt as all its associations were with the criminal underworld. The Jewish historian Josephus noted that the governor of Judea, Florus, was regarded as exceptionally cruel because he had even Jews of high rank scourged and crucified. All the circumstances of crucifixion added to the degradation of the condemned prisoner. He had to carry his cross (probably the crossbeam, the horizontal arm) by a prominent route to the place of execution so that the maximum number of people could see his shame. His crime was written on a placard carried before him and then fixed to his cross as a warning to other would-be offenders. The execution site was usually on the side of a public road so that the casual passer-by could not help seeing the dying felon. He was stripped of his clothes before being nailed or tied to the cross so that he hung in public view deprived of normal human dignity.

In view of the extreme torture involved in crucifixion, the accompanying humiliation might seem a minor annoyance, but it added considerably to the sufferings of the condemned criminal. The amount of pain one feels depends partly on psychological factors and to take away the sufferer's dignity makes the pain harder to bear. Contempt and cruelty often go together and oppressors either deliberately or instinctively use both to keep their victims in subjection. In the battle of wills between the one inflicting pain and the one who bears it, humiliation is an additional weapon the torturer uses to establish his own superiority and perhaps silence any whispers of conscience which may stir in him. Modern enlightened governments outlaw torture and degrading punishments. It is significant that these two go together because many regimes have cynically used both as instruments of repression.

The gospels record the humiliations which Jesus suffered from the time of his arrest in the garden to his death and the Reproaches have many allusions to them, but especially when they state:

> you struck me down and scourged me ...
> you struck my head with a reed ...
> you gave me a crown of thorns.

The following words in the passion narratives (all taken from the same translation so as not to exaggerate their number) describe the insults and pains Jesus suffered: 'laid hands on', 'arrested', 'spat on', 'struck', 'slapped', 'bound', 'led away', 'handed him over', 'accused', 'shouted ... "Let him be crucified"', 'flogged', 'stripped', 'divided his clothes ... casting lots to decide what each should take', 'derided', 'taunted', 'condemned as deserving death', 'blindfolded', 'beat', 'seized', 'heaped insults', 'treated with contempt', 'crucified... with the criminals', 'scoffed'. It is scarcely possible to separate insult from pain in the treatment Jesus suffered from his arrest till his death; he was both mocked and scourged, but we shall look first at the shameful aspect of his passion. There was a greater or less degree of deliberate mockery of Christ in all the events from Gethsemane till he breathed his last on the cross. To be arrested is itself humiliating. Jesus was seized and bound in the garden by a crowd armed with swords and clubs and marched in bonds to the high priest's palace. After the Sanhedrin had condemned him as worthy of death, some of its members, or those hanging around, indulged their venom against him with jeers, taunts and blows. They spat on him and struck him. They played crude practical jokes by blindfolding him, cuffing him and asking him to prophesy who had hit him. We can imagine the inane taunting which would accompany this horse play as they recalled Jesus' reputation as prophet. In the middle of the trial by Pilate, Luke records that the governor sent him to Herod the tetrarch who, with his soldiers, 'treated him with contempt and mocked him' (Lk 23:11). Herod refused to condemn him to death but sent him back to Pilate dressed in a splendid robe, probably in mockery.

After Pilate had passed sentence on Jesus and handed him over to his soldiers for crucifixion they treated him as a figure of fun. These soldiers were probably not the crack troops of the Roman army but recruits drawn from surrounding countries and likely to be anti-Jewish. Knowing that Jesus had been condemned to death for his alleged claim to be 'King of the Jews' they took the opportunity to ridicule him and the Jews by dressing him up as a king. They bowed before him with the mocking salutation 'Hail!', in parody of the way they were accustomed to salute the Emperor. They hastily knocked together a circlet of thorn branches and stuck it on his head. They placed a reed in his hand as sceptre. Their buffoonery turned brutal when they cuffed him on the face and, seizing the reed from his hands, struck him with it over the head. Their behaviour was callous and typical of the ordinary brutality of army life at the time. It probably did not show personal malice against Jesus and may have been a way of coping with the boredom of their job. They were soldiers doing largely police duties in an occupied country, no doubt thoroughly detested by the people and returning this feeling in equal measure. To some extent they were victims of the system, of the politics of the region and of inherited racial hatreds. The passion of Christ was caused by a great variety of sins, ranging widely in their gravity and compounded by the corporate sin of the human race. Racism with its accompanying injustice and contempt were among the evils which crucified our Saviour.

The mockery of Christ by both Jews and Romans continued when he hung on the cross. Crowds had gathered to see the crucifixions of the three condemned men, just as later in history they went to public hangings. As well as that, the crosses stood beside a public road so that passers-by could not avoid seeing this gruesome form of capital punishment. Many of the public taunted Jesus on his cruel fate and no doubt jeered at the two robbers as well. Some members of the Sanhedrin gloated over him as the helpless 'king' who could not save himself and challenged him that if he came down from the cross then they would believe in him. Even the robbers, his fellow victims, taunted him in similar terms (Mt.27:44, Mk 15:32), though Luke recorded that one of the two disagreed with his companion and asked Jesus 'remember me when you come into your kingdom' (Lk 23:42).

The Roman soldiers who carried out the horrible act of crucifixion showed some elements of kindness when they offered Jesus some drugged wine, which he refused, at the beginning of his ordeal (Mk 15:23) and gave him their normal drink of sour wine at the end (Mk 15:36). The centurion also confessed Christ's innocence after he died (Mk 15:39, Lk 23:47). Yet Luke portrayed the soldiers as joining in the taunts of the crowd and the offer of wine as mock homage. 'The soldiers also mocked him, coming up and offering him sour wine, and saying, "If you are the king of the Jews, save yourself!"' (Lk 23:36-37). The description suggests that they came forward with a mocking bow as if to a king with some such sneering words as, 'Would your majesty like a drink?' The element of mockery in this action is not so pronounced in Matthew and Mark but neither is it absent. In contrast to Luke, the first two gospels connect the offer of sour wine with the cry of dereliction, 'My God, my God, why have you forsaken me?' Some of those at the cross thought that Jesus was calling for Elijah and the offer of cheap, unpalatable wine drew attention to the helplessness of Christ who had no Elijah to come and help him. Hence even the minimal kindness of the soldiers probably had an element of contempt, as when a coin of little value is carelessly thrown to a beggar.

Jesus Tortured

The Reproaches explicitly mention the crown of thorns and the reed, which we have taken as summary examples of all the humiliation Christ suffered in his passion. They also twice refer to the scourging of Jesus: 'You brought your scourges down on me.' 'You struck me down and scourged me.' They probably understand the word as describing the whole suffering which Christ endured, but certainly including the specific punishment of the lash. Mocking and scourging go together, as mockery which arises from malice almost inevitably becomes physical abuse, taunting words lead to vicious blows. The Reproaches' use of the word 'down' in connection with Christ's scourging brings out its degrading nature as well as the agony it inflicted. The victim was thrown on the ground or over a frame so that the lashes would fall on his back as both torture and humiliation. In addition to the partly incidental violence of cruel joking, Christ suffered the deliberate, carefully regulated ordeal of scourging with its high degree of physical pain. In an age when corporal punishment has largely been abolished, modern readers of the gospels may not fully grasp what a Roman flogging involved.

Different kinds of beatings are mentioned in the New Testament with a wide range of severity. When Paul and Silas were arrested in Philippi they were beaten with rods before being thrown into the local jail (Acts 16:22-23). This was a humiliating and painful punishment but did not usually entail serious injury. Scourging was much more cruel. (Strictly speaking there were three kinds of whipping in the Roman Empire, beating, flogging and scourging, in that order of severity, but it is doubtful if the New Testament writers distinguish between the latter two.) When Paul was rescued from a Jerusalem mob by the Roman tribune the latter intended to torture him by scourging to find out the truth of his dispute with the Jews, but Paul escaped this dreadful ordeal by announcing that he was a Roman citizen (Acts 22:24). No Roman citizen was subjected to scourging. Like crucifixion, it was reserved for slaves and foreigners. The scourge consisted of leather thongs to which were attached bits of bone or metal, probably similar to the cat o' nine tails once used in the British Navy. The victim's flesh was lacerated by this fearful weapon so that men sometimes died from being flogged. Scourging could be used to extract confessions, as the tribune intended doing to Paul. It was also part of the punishment of crucifixion, as we noted in the case of Florus' treatment of his Jewish opponents. According to the first two gospels, Jesus was flogged as a preliminary to his crucifixion (Mt 27:26, Mk 15:15). John placed the flogging in the middle of the trial, before sentence was passed (Jn 19:1). Luke did not actually say that Jesus was scourged but he represented Pilate as trying (unsuccessfully) to persuade the crowds that that would be a sufficient punishment (Lk 23:16, 22-23). Whatever may be the details, we can be confident that Jesus underwent the horror of a Roman flogging as part of his passion.

Christ's Identification with the Oppressed

The Reproaches contrast the cruel, insulting behaviour people meted out to Jesus with the care God showed to his people by destroying their enemies, feeding them with manna and giving them 'a royal sceptre'.

> For your sake I scourged your captors and first-born sons,
> but you brought your scourges down on me.
>
> I bore you up with manna in the desert,
> but you struck me down and scourged me.
> For you I struck down the kings of Canaan,

but you struck my head with a reed.
I gave you a royal sceptre,
but you gave me a crown of thorns.

We must first deal with the hostility to and apparent lack of pity for Israel's enemies. As we noted in an earlier chapter, much of the Old Testament quite unselfconsciously portrays God as the one who rescued his people by destroying their oppressors. The defeat of evil entails facing up to the enormity of evil and this must include the overthrow of oppressive power. But evil and injustice in human society are rarely straightforward and their remedies are often a mixture of good and bad. The children of Israel were victims in Egypt but acted as aggressors in the conquest of Canaan. A radical solution to the human predicament cannot simply be a change round in the positions of oppressor and oppressed, but must involve the rescue of both from the corporate evil which enslaves them. The significant thing about the Reproaches is that in them Jesus is identified with the sufferings of Israel's enemies. He is their fellow victim, not the one who punishes them, and his patient bearing of the pain human beings inflict on each other opens up the way to reconciliation with God and peace with justice on earth.

The care which God showed his people by defeating their enemies, feeding them with manna and giving them a 'royal sceptre', may be summarised as giving them a sense of their true dignity and worth. The rescue from Egypt foreshadows the liberty Christ won for humanity by his cross, by his enduring the pains and insults we human beings inflicted on him. 'You' in the Reproaches always represents the human race as a whole. All of us, Jews and Gentiles together, mocked Jesus and his bearing of this mockery is part of God's work in restoring us to true humanity. Cruel jeering at the helpless often indicates something deeply amiss in the scoffer. It may reveal a degree of self-loathing, a pathetic attempt to compensate for low self-esteem by pouring insults on some other unfortunate person. God in Christ absorbs the venom of human self-hate and the cruelty towards others which is often its consequence, and he gives us, if we respond to his love, peace with God, with others and with ourselves. By our sinful lives, and in particular by our contempt for those in any way disadvantaged, or by our sheer neglect of them, we mock Christ, the king of kings, with a crown of thorns, jeering homage and blows on the head with a reed as a mock sceptre. Repentance means that we receive from Christ, with trembling and shame, his true royal sceptre and reign with him seated in the courts of heaven.

Along with the mocking went the deliberate torture of a Roman flogging. We can see in Christ's endurance of this cruel practice his identification with all who have suffered torture and degrading punishment throughout the centuries, not least in the present time. In spite of the lip service paid to the principle of humane treatment of prisoners, torture is still widely practised, not only by terrorist groups who dominate communities through fear but even by official government authorities in some lands. Totalitarian regimes use torture systematically and extensively, aided by scientific techniques which can refine it to greater intensity. It is combined with humiliation as a deliberate ploy to cow resistance, hold a community in the grip of terror and sap the will to resist an oppressor. The treatment meted out to Jesus was crude and brutal, lacking the sophistication of modern refinements in torture but similar in kind. Christ by his scourging and crucifixion identified himself with the oppressed, the degraded and the tortured, the victims of the world's cruelty. He bore these with all other sins in his passion and, by his patient acceptance of suffering, opened up the way to victory over sin, both for the oppressor and the oppressed.

The Truth behind the Mockery and Scourging

Many a true word is spoken in jest and Christ's mockers paid tribute to his royal dignity without knowing what they were saying or doing. The soldiers thought it a good joke to stick a bundle of thorns on Christ's head as a crown but did not realise that he was indeed their king and the painful, shameful crown of thorns was a sign of the royal victory of suffering love over the pathetic and, in the long run, futile efforts of human beings to bolster up their pride at the expense of others' dignity. Their words 'Hail, King of the Jews', accompanied by mocking genuflections, parodied their act of respect to Caesar and unconsciously transferred the allegiance to its true owner. The title on the cross, 'The king of the Jews', was meant to indicate Jesus' crime, but it described his rightful position and indeed did not go far enough since Christ is king of the universe. The jeering religious leaders at the cross also gave the same unconscious homage to Jesus when they scoffed, 'He saved others; he cannot save himself' (Mk 15:31). They spoke more truly than they knew, as when Caiaphas said, 'It is better for you to have one man die for the people than to have the whole nation destroyed' (Jn 11:50). Only by not saving himself could Jesus atone for the sins of the world and save humankind in a radical way of which his works of healing were anticipatory signs. Christ chose to be weak and vulnerable in the face of human pride, cruelty, injustice and contempt. 'Let the Messiah, the King of Israel, come down from the cross now, so that we may see and believe' (Mk 15:32). He had already rejected Satan's temptation to throw himself down from the pinnacle of the temple and win a following by a spectacular display of superhuman power over death. He did not invoke divine omnipotence to descend from the cross, confound his enemies and win their allegiance through terror. 'He trusts in God; let God deliver him now, if he wants to; for he said, "I am God's Son"' (Mt 27:43). Christ on the cross trusted in his Father with naked faith, in the absence of any outward assurance of God's power. He cried out, 'My God, my God, why have you forsaken me?' in the words of the same Psalm where the writer also hears the taunting words of his enemies, 'Commit your cause to the Lord; let him deliver – let him rescue the one in whom he delights!' (Ps 22:8). Christ bore the sarcastic jibes of those who, in their mockery of faith, unconsciously revealed its true nature, clinging to God when he seems absent and every circumstance of life makes for despair. Christ identifies himself with the honest doubter in a bleak world and with the anguished cry of many in all ages, 'Why has this happened to me?' Because he is one with sin's victims he can give them victory over the evil in the world and in themselves.

Insults have a way of rebounding on those who make them and becoming a badge of honour for the ones insulted. It is claimed that in the First World War the British expeditionary force in France was described by the Kaiser as a 'contemptible little army'. The title 'the Old Contemptibles' has now become a name proudly borne by a diminishing number of survivors from that war. Roman soldiers were accustomed to salute their commander by bowing on one knee, a genuflection. They performed this action before Jesus hanging on the cross as a mockery. The Roman legions are no more but many Christians now use this act of respect when they come forward to receive Holy Communion or reverence the Blessed Sacrament. God can transform our mockery and our hate so that through repentance we learn true respect for him and for our fellow human beings.

St Paul described his preaching of Christ crucified as 'a stumbling block to Jews and folly to Gentiles' (1 Cor 1:23). The mocking and scourging of Christ show very clearly what an offence the crucifixion was to the Jewish sense of God's power and the Greek pride in human wisdom. Paul was writing to the Corinthian Christians who were prone to admire spectacular displays of eloquence, to prize the more showy spiritual gifts and to enjoy the excitement of partisan disputes in their assemblies. In opposition to that kind of behaviour and thinking, he held before them the crucified Christ, the negation of human pride. He showed them in Christ the wisdom of God which exposes self-confident human wisdom as folly and the strength of God which conquers human might by its weakness. The weakness of Jesus on the cross is not the fearful cringing of a slave before a cruel master; it is his willing acceptance of the fate of the oppressed in order to break their yoke. Following Christ's example does not mean that it is our duty to let other people trample over us and make us feel like dirt. But neither is human dignity and self-worth achieved by increasing our own power at the expense of others or by trying to make ourselves important by downgrading others. Our highest dignity is found by our union with the crucified and risen Christ. He submitted to the scourging and mocking of the fearful, self-important and cruel sides of human nature and, by doing so, achieved the re-creation of humanity in the image of God. Our tendency to injure and scoff at other people often betrays insecurity and self-hate in ourselves which we then project on to others. Both the victims and perpetrators of cruelty need healing. Christ, in his perfect manhood, met the concentrated hate of fallen humanity without being embittered by it or hating his torturers in return, but with steadfast love in all his agony. Christ won by his passion a new dignity for the human race, based on the victory of love over hate, faith over fear, and confidence as God's children over the degrading force of sin.

A minor, though telling, example of how Christ's crucifixion has changed human outlook is the position the cross now holds in human speech and art. To appreciate the great extent of this change we have to remember the utter horror which the cross had in the Roman Empire, and that includes the time when Paul was writing to the early Christians about glorying in the cross of Christ. Many Roman authors show the disgust and shame which the cross aroused in them, and in the centuries immediately following Christ's life, opponents of Christianity frequently poured scorn on Christian worship of a crucified man. One of the earliest representations of the crucifixion is a blasphemous graffito excavated in an ancient palace on the Palatine Hill in Rome. It depicts a rough cross with an ass's head fixed to it and a figure in an attitude of prayer in front of it. Underneath are scrawled in semi-literate Greek the words, 'Alexamenos worships his god'. It was probably the work of a slave mocking the religion of a fellow slave who was a Christian. Contrast this mocking sketch with the later development of the cross in Christian art. While a gold or silver cross adorning a church may disguise the brutal reality of the crucifixion, it also shows that this shameful instrument of torture is transformed into the means of human redemption. God, through his love for sinful humanity, has changed one of the worst examples of cruelty into a symbol of conquering, forgiving love. We proclaim this transformation in hymns like 'Lift high the cross', or the chorus of *Pange lingua* in the Reproaches:

> Faithful Cross! above all other,
> One and only noble tree!
> None in foliage, none in blossom,
> None in fruit thy peer may be;
> Sweetest wood and sweetest iron!
> Sweetest weight is hung on thee.

However, the real transformation effected by Christ's cross is in the lives of people who have found meaning and dignity through their contact with the crucified and risen Saviour. Christ became the victim of human sin and one with fallen humanity in its separation from God when he hung on the cross. In this action he destroyed the power of evil and opened up the way to reconciliation with God. He offers us a new identity as forgiven sinners, a status from which we can grow into a new humanity alive with the life of God.

CHAPTER 5

The Thirst of Christ

The Drink of Wine

All four gospels refer to Christ being offered something to drink during his crucifixion, and Matthew and Mark mention this as happening twice. The first time he was offered wine (*oinos*) mixed with myrrh (Mk 15:23) or gall (Mt 27:34), which he refused. It was a humane practice to give those condemned to be crucified a drink of wine to lessen the pain. The usual explanation (and the most probable) why Jesus refused this drink is that he wished to make his passion an offering to God with a clear head, though some scholars think that Mark understood him to reject any reduction in his sufferings. The second time Jesus was offered a drink on the cross, according to Matthew and Mark, was near the moment of death and the drink offered was sour wine or vinegar (*oxos*), the cheap wine which Roman soldiers commonly drank. Both Matthew and Mark say this offer was in response to Christ's cry of dereliction, 'My God, my God, why have you forsaken me?' It is possible that a soldier or bystander offered the dying Christ this drink out of compassion for his raging thirst, but it could have been done at least partly out of mockery, as we noted in the previous chapter. Luke does not connect the offering of wine with the cry of dereliction but explicitly states that it was done in mockery (Lk 23:36-37).

Two of the Reproaches follow Matthew, Mark and Luke in treating the offer of sour wine to Jesus on the cross as a hostile act.

> What more could I have done for you?
> I planted you as my fairest vine,
> but you yielded only bitterness:
> when I was thirsty you gave me vinegar to drink ...
> I gave you saving water from the rock,
> but you gave me gall and vinegar to drink.

According to this understanding, the thirst of Christ was part of his physical pain and the offer of sour wine added insult to injury. The form of the gospel accounts, followed closely by the Reproaches, is strongly influenced by the Psalms, showing that the torture Christ endured on the cross is the fulfilment of the sufferings experienced by the innocent faithful servants of God in the Old Testament. Jesus uttered his cry of dereliction in the opening words of Psalm 22, 'My God, my God, why have you forsaken me?' and in a later verse we read:

> My mouth is dried up like a potsherd,
> and my tongue sticks to my jaws (v. 15).

Similarly in Psalm 69 the author pours out his anguish,

> I am weary with my crying; my throat is parched (v.3),

and,

> They gave me poison for food,
> and for my thirst they gave me vinegar to drink (v. 21).

St John, however, in his passion narrative, has a further understanding of the thirst of Christ and the offer of a drink:

> After this, when Jesus knew that all was now fulfilled (*tetelestai*), he said (in order to fulfil (*teleióthé*) the scripture), 'I am thirsty.' A jar full of sour wine was standing there. So they put a sponge full of the wine on a branch of hyssop and held it to his mouth. When Jesus had received the wine, he said, 'It is finished (*Tetelestai*).' Then he bowed his head and gave up his spirit (Jn 19:28-30).

Various forms of the same word in Greek, translated 'fulfil' or 'finish', occur three times in this short passage. John alone recorded the word from the cross, 'I am thirsty' and he saw the thirst of Jesus both as a fulfilment of scripture and also as marking the completion and climax of Christ's work of salvation since it is associated with his last great triumphal shout, 'It is finished'.

Thirst and Hunger in the Old and New Testaments

The word 'I am thirsty' is not an exact quotation from the Old Testament, so we are encouraged to see in it a fulfilment of the Jewish scripture as a whole rather than of any one particular passage. Thirst, hunger, food and drink are common biblical themes and to explore them yields important insights into

Christ's work on the cross. The Reproaches refer to some of the passages dealing with these themes and connect them with Christ's passion. In addition to the two noted above, we have the Reproach,

> I bore you up with manna in the desert,
> but you struck me down and scourged me.

The agony of Christ's passion, and in particular his thirst, is contrasted with God's loving provision for his people in their desert wanderings and his continued care for them in the promised land. This care is symbolised by the gift of manna and of water from the rock. The gift of water is more closely related to Christ's thirst and more prominent in the Reproaches, but manna is also important as it had a major place in Jewish folk memory, and its symbolism for God's care is developed in the New Testament. The Psalms often retell the exodus story in the form of praise to God, and his supply of manna to the wandering Israelites is a recurring theme (e.g. Ps 78:23-24; 105:40). The ark of the Lord was believed to contain a jar of manna (Ex 16:33). Over the centuries there developed the idea of manna as heavenly food, 'the bread of angels' (Ps 78:25), and it came to be associated with the age of the Messiah. The Jews of our Lord's time referred to Moses' provision of manna to their ancestors according to St John's account of their dispute with him (Jn 6:31-32, 49), which leads into the discourse where Christ describes himself as 'the bread of life', food for the world provided by his death (Jn 6:51). In the last book of the New Testament there is a cryptic reference to the 'hidden manna' which will be given to faithful Christians (Rev 2:17).

God's care of his people on their exodus journey, of which the gift of manna is a potent symbol, often met with grumbling or rejection on their part. God provided them with the manna when they were filled with self-pity and ready to go back to Egypt because they had no food (Ex 16:3,15). Even though it kept them alive they became tired of it after a time and started to complain again and to hanker after the delicacies of Egypt (Num 11:4-6). The story of God's people in the Old Testament is, among other things, a record of rebellion and rejection of God's care. The New Testament sees the climax and supreme example of this rejection in the crucifixion of Christ. Stephen, the first Christian martyr, in his speech before the Sanhedrin, recounted the history of Israel in such a way as to show how God's people repeatedly spurned his care and his servants (Acts 7:2-53), yet in spite of, and even by means of, their wrong-doing God carried out his plan to save them. Joseph's brothers were jealous of him, sold him as a slave into Egypt, and through that action God saved his people and the surrounding nations from famine. Many generations later, the whole nation became enslaved in Egypt and when Moses appeared as God's deliverer they repeatedly rebuffed him. 'He supposed that his kinsfolk would understand that God through him was rescuing them, but they did not understand' (v. 25). 'Our ancestors were unwilling to obey him; instead, they pushed him aside, and in their hearts they turned back to Egypt' (v. 39). Later they rejected God's prophets and in the end handed Christ over to be crucified. The implication is that through this action God will bring about the salvation of all his people, Jews and Gentiles together. The Reproaches take up the thought that God's people repeatedly reject his care for them and those he sends to save them, yet through their rejection his saving purpose is fulfilled in a way they could never have imagined.

I bore you up with manna in the desert,
but you struck me down and scourged me.

God's gift of manna is fulfilled in the heavenly manna, the bread of life, which we receive in Christ. But it was only through the betrayal, torture and death of Christ that his life is available to us. Just as grain has to be threshed, ground into flour and baked in an oven to become bread, so Christ's body endured the scourging and agony of the cross in order that he might become food for the world. When we receive the bread of life in Holy Communion we make the memorial of Christ's sacrifice on the cross because it is only through the cross that we are fed with Christ's body and blood and given a share in his risen life. 'For as often as you eat this bread and drink the cup, you proclaim the Lord's death until he comes' (1 Cor 11:26).

Manna satisfied the hunger of the children of Israel on their journey; God also relieved their thirst when, according to their tradition, he commanded Moses to strike a rock and make it a spring of water (Ex 17:1-7. Num 20:2-13). Thirst is an even more severe trial than hunger. People like the Israelites who lived in dry countries in ancient times were very familiar with being thirsty and often experienced the agonising desire for water. Hence thirst is a powerful and much used metaphor in the Bible to express deep longing. Water also is a fitting symbol of God's grace in answer to the deepest human need.

As a deer longs for flowing streams,
so my soul longs for you, O God.
My soul thirsts for God,
for the living God.
When shall I come and behold
the face of God? (Ps 42:1-2).

O God, you are my God, I seek you,
my soul thirsts for you;
my flesh faints for you,
as in a dry and weary land where there is no water (Ps 63:1).

Jesus spoke of the happiness of 'those who hunger and thirst for righteousness' (Mt 5:6). He described himself as the source of the living water of eternal life (Jn 4:14). On the feast of tabernacles he cried out to the people in the temple courts, 'Let anyone who is thirsty come to me, and let the one who believes in me drink' (Jn 7:37-38). The evangelist commented that he was speaking of the Holy Spirit who could only be given after Jesus was 'glorified', that is, crucified and risen (v. 39). Like the bread of life, the gift of the water of life, which is the Holy Spirit, can only reach us through Christ's passion. Christ's words echo God's invitation through his prophet,

Ho, everyone who thirsts,
come to the waters;
and you who have no money,
come, buy and eat!
Come, buy wine and milk
without money and without price (Isa 55:1).

The food and drink which are eternal life are God's free gift to us, free because we can do nothing to earn it, but infinitely costly to God because it requires the passion of his Son.

'I am Thirsty'

All these and other similar references lie behind Christ's word on the cross, 'I am thirsty', which John comments was to fulfil the scripture (Jn 19:28). It indicates first of all the physical pain which Christ endured in obeying his Father's will. The torture he went through on the cross, as we noted earlier, fulfils the sufferings of the innocent in the Old Testament. Even the drink of sour wine given to him may have had an element of contempt, emphasising his helplessness on the cross. Christ identified himself with the helpless victims of man's inhumanity to man, including the humiliation which sometimes accompanies help given to the needy. This is one of the many sins for which he makes atonement.

The thirst of Christ on the cross is more than his physical pain. 'Thirst', as we noted, is a metaphor in the Bible for our longing to know God and to do his will, a longing which Christ satisfies through his death. Christ shared our thirst for God during his life on earth and longed to do his will in a way far beyond our normal desires. The happiness of those who hunger and thirst for righteousness was his in full measure. He said, 'My food is to do the will of him who sent me and to complete his work' (Jn 4:34). Yet because he identified himself with us in our fallen state, the doing of God's will became for him a hard, agonising task so that he prayed to God in Gethsemane, 'Remove this cup from me; yet, not what I want, but what you want' (Mk 14:36). Just as Jesus could only give himself to us as the bread of life by giving up his life in death, so he could only satisfy our thirst for the water of eternal life by drinking to its dregs the cup of suffering which was obedience to God under the conditions of being identified with sinful humanity.

Christ's thirst both indicates the climax of his sufferings on the cross and also the fulfilment of God's plan of salvation as it unfolds throughout the Old Testament. St John tells the story of the passion in such a way as to bring out the eternal purpose of God which is the hidden reality behind the sordid, brutal act of crucifixion. He gives the saying 'I am thirsty' to show Christ's desire to do his Father's will and to complete the task he had been given on earth. All the participants in Christ's passion, from the Jewish leaders who condemned him to the Roman soldiers who crucified him, are brought into God's eternal plan. The action of the soldiers in giving the dying Jesus a drink of sour wine connects them with the deeper meaning of his thirst. There is no hint of contempt in John's account of their action. At the human level, it makes sense as a kindly act of relief for a dying man's thirst. But John was more interested in its deeper significance.

Earlier in his account of the arrest of Jesus, he noted that when Peter drew his sword and struck a servant of the high priest Jesus said to him, 'Put your sword back into its sheath. Am I not to drink the cup that the Father has given me ?' (Jn 18:11). The soldiers at the cross, all unknowingly, were assisting Jesus in drinking to the last drop the cup of suffering which was the climax of his thirst to perform his Father's will for the salvation of the world. The water of life which Jesus gives us was purchased at the cost of his thirst on the cross, understanding his thirst as his whole passion. The Reproaches speak of the 'saving water from the rock' which God through Moses gave to the thirsty Israelites. St Paul commenting on this episode stated, 'They drank from the spiritual rock that followed them, and the rock was Christ' (1 Cor 10:4). The water from the rock saved the Israelites from a painful death, but when we use the words in our Good Friday worship we can understand them with Paul as referring to the water of salvation given to us through Christ's death on the cross. He suffered the thirst of death so that our thirst might be quenched. The Reproaches contrast the gracious act of God with our cruel response. It was by enduring the world's cruelty with patient redeeming love that Christ made available to us the water of eternal life.

The Spear Thrust

> When I was thirsty you gave me vinegar to drink,
> and you pierced your Saviour with a lance.
>
> I opened the sea before you,
> but you opened my side with a spear.

The spear thrust into the side of the dead Christ is another detail only found in John's passion narrative. The Reproaches take it as a further humiliation of Christ in the dishonour of his dead body but, while that is their main thought, the spear thrust immediately brings to mind the blood and water which flowed from Christ's side. There has been a wealth of speculation about the blood and water with many fanciful interpretations of their meaning, but John clearly wishes his readers to see these details as significant. He recorded the event 'so that you also may believe' (Jn 19:35) and, in view of the concerns of his gospel as a whole, 'believe' cannot refer only to mere fact but must relate to deeper reality. He noted that it happened 'so that the scripture might be fulfilled' (v. 36) and this confirms his interest in the inner meaning of the blood and water. We can safely interpret these symbols in the light of his earlier reference to Jesus as the one who gives 'living water' and who makes those who believe in him themselves springs of living water (Jn 4:14; 7:38). The water of eternal life is given through the outpouring of the Spirit (Jn 7:39) and that is only possible through the death of Jesus. The flowing of water and blood from Christ's side after his death is a very vivid symbol of the gift of life in the Spirit through his death. Christ gave up his life blood in order to share it with us. He had described his coming passion as a 'cup' and a 'baptism' (Mk 10:38). The baptism becomes a baptism in the Spirit because Jesus underwent a baptism of blood to give us his Spirit. We can drink of the cup of salvation because Jesus first drank the cup of suffering. The thirst of Christ quenches our thirst. It is fully in keeping with the general tenor of John's gospel to understand the water and blood which flowed from Christ's side as signifying Christ's life given to us through his death and, by a further extension of meaning, as referring to the sacraments of baptism and the eucharist. Through faith and through these sacraments we become one with Christ in his death and resurrection. John drew attention to the water and blood 'so that you also may believe'. He is clearly speaking of the saving faith by which we are united with Christ.

The scripture fulfilled by the spear thrust of Christ is 'They will look on the one whom they have pierced' (Jn 19:37, quoting Zech 12:10). The full verse reads:

> And I will pour a spirit of compassion and supplication on the house of David and the inhabitants of Jerusalem, so that, when they look on the one whom they have pierced, they shall mourn for him, as one mourns for an only child, and weep bitterly over him, as one weeps over a firstborn.

Zechariah understood that the effect of seeing the pierced body of the one unjustly punished was to cause a change of heart. Those who pierced him now mourn and weep for him because God poured out on them 'a spirit of compassion and supplication'. The phrase 'I will pour out' links the prophecy with the flow of blood and water from the spear-pierced side of Christ. The prophet went on to describe the intensity of mourning and implied that it included penitence. 'On that day a fountain shall be opened for the house of David and the inhabitants of Jerusalem, to cleanse them from sin and iniquity' (Zech 13:1). The evangelist uses the words of the prophet and their context to invite us, his readers in every age, to see in Christ who was pierced for us the saviour and life-giver who changes our hearts and empowers us with new life. The intention of the Reproaches is similar – to make us see in the sufferings of Christ the result of our sins and their remedy.

Zechariah's words are also found in the book of Revelation which throws further light on their connection with Christ's passion and our response to it.

> Look! He is coming with the clouds;
> every eye will see him,
> even those who pierced him;
> and on his account all the tribes of the earth will wail
> (Rev 1:7).

The author envisaged Christ in his final judgement revealing to all humanity the marks of his passion which will convict us of what we have done to our Saviour. This final judgement is foreshadowed in the soldier who stabbed Christ's body with his spear and the bystanders who saw what happened. In the book of Revelation the sight of Christ who is pierced is meant to be both a comfort to a persecuted, suffering church and also a warning to all sinful people. If we apply the passage to other ages and places, we should heed both the comfort and the warning. In so far as God's people suffer for their faith, Christ has suffered with them. In so far as they are sinful (a universal condition), they have inflicted suffering on Christ and the sight of his pierced body is intended to bring sorrow leading to repentance. The final coming of Christ throws its light backward into the present and every other age, so that we can now experience in foretaste his judgement and mercy. The Reproach, therefore, is a salutary and healing one which we can apply to ourselves:

> I planted you as my fairest vine,
> but you yielded only bitterness:
> when I was thirsty you gave me vinegar to drink,
> and you pierced your Saviour with a lance.

Christ the Vine

The Reproaches connect the thirst of Christ with another basic idea of the Bible, Israel as God's vine. When the theme occurs there is usually a contrast between God's loving care for his vine and its miserable return for his care. Jeremiah wrote,

> Yet I planted you as a choice vine,
> from the purest stock.
> How then did you turn degenerate
> and become a wild vine? (Jer 2:21)

The theme is more fully worked out in Isaiah 5:1-7, the well-known parable of the vineyard which God planted in fertile soil. He cleared the ground of stones, he planted it with choice vines and he built a watch tower for its protection. Everything favoured a bumper crop of fine grapes but, to the owner's bitter disappointment, all that the vineyard produced was wild grapes. The Reproaches connect the wild grapes of the parable with the vinegar given in mockery to Christ on the cross. The bitterness of God's disappointment at his people's disobedience foreshadowed the bitterness of Christ's cruel death. In Isaiah the owner of the vineyard threatened in his anger to lay it waste:

> I will remove its hedge,
> and it shall be devoured;
> I will break down its wall,
> and it shall be trampled down.
> I will make it a waste;
> it shall not be pruned or hoed,
> and it shall be overgrown with briers and thorns;
> I will also command the clouds
> that they rain no rain upon it (Isa 5:5-6).

But Christ himself bore the dire consequences of God's people's failure to bear the fruit of obedience.

Christ told a parable clearly related to the theme of Israel as God's vineyard, the parable of the wicked tenant farmers (Mk 12:1-12, Mt 21:33-46, Lk 20:9-19). The vineyard owner, in words which echo Isaiah's story, made every provision for a good yield of grapes. He 'put a fence around it' (Mk 12:1) so that the wild beasts would not trample over the vines. He 'dug a pit for the wine press' so that the tenants had the necessary equipment to make good wine. He 'built a watchtower' so that one of them could keep a lookout to protect the vineyard from thieves. Yet the tenants kept all the produce for themselves and illtreated every servant of the owner who came to collect the owner's just share. 'Finally' (Mk 12:6), as the fulfilment of the vineyard's history, the owner sent his son. But the tenants saw a chance to gain outright possession of the vineyard and murdered the rightful heir 'and threw him out of the vineyard' (v. 8), a significant detail in view of Christ's shameful death outside the walls of the holy city Jerusalem.

Another Old Testament passage which speaks of Israel as God's vine, Psalm 80, throws further light on this theme. The psalm is an impassioned prayer to God by a people groaning under the scorn and oppression of their enemies, which could fit many periods of Israel's history. The author recounted the story of God's rescue of the people from Egypt and his subsequent care of them in the promised land under the same figure as Isaiah used, a vine on which the owner lavished all his attention:

> You brought a vine out of Egypt;
> you drove out the nations and planted it.
> You cleared the ground for it;
> it took deep root and filled the land (Ps 80:8-9).

The greatness of the vine is described with poetic exaggeration as overshadowing the mountains and the mighty cedars, and stretching from the sea (the Mediterranean) to the river (the Euphrates) (vv. 10-11). Then the tone changes abruptly. In the characteristic Old Testament way we have already noted, the psalmist bitterly asked God:

> Why then have you broken down its walls,
> so that all who pass along the way pluck its fruit?
> The boar from the forest ravages it,
> and all that move in the field feed on it (vv. 12-13).

He went on to plead that God would turn again with favour on his beloved vine and restore it to its former prosperity.

Psalm 80 represents the cry of God's people under the oppressor's yoke. Christ in his passion identified himself with their cry. He bore the sufferings both of the innocent and the guilty in order to make possible the restoration of humanity to the state God intends for it. The psalm's account of the nation's oppression fittingly describes both the pain Christ endured and also his humiliation.

> You have fed [your people] with the bread of tears,
> and given them tears to drink in full measure.

You make us the scorn of our neighbours;
our enemies laugh among themselves (Ps 80:5-6).

The psalmist goes on to plead with God to look with favour on the nation's woes, destroy its oppressors and restore its fortunes to the good old days of David and Solomon:

Turn again, O God of hosts;
look down from heaven and see;
have regard for this vine,
the stock that your right hand planted.
They have burned it with fire, they have cut it down;
may they perish at the rebuke of your countenance.
But let your hand be upon the one at your right hand,
the one whom you made strong for your self.
Then we will never turn back from you;
give us life, and we will call upon your name (vv. 14-18).

Through the sacrifice of Christ, God answered the psalmist's prayer and that of all the oppressed in a way much greater and more fundamental than they could have imagined. He identified himself with the oppressed and willingly accepted death on the cross, but this should not be interpreted as urging the world's victims of injustice to be content with their lot. Christ by his sufferings offered both oppressor and oppressed freedom from the enslaving forces which bound them and this freedom includes the creation of a new society where all can live with the dignity of the redeemed children of God.

Christ described himself as 'the true vine' (Jn 15:1), clearly bringing together the many references to Israel as God's vine or vineyard in the Old Testament. His life showed the fruits which God expected from Israel but often failed to receive. Yet he suffered the fate of the vine which the Old Testament authors variously describe as the wicked attacks of Israel's enemies and as God's punishment of his people for their sins. Through his passion Christ restored God's vine to what God had called his people to be. He was most fully the true vine when he died on the cross obeying God to the uttermost. He invites all to become branches of the vine by faith in him. His thirst to complete God's saving will for the world, which included the agony of the cross, satisfies the thirst of humanity for significance and value, for the water of life, however dim or misplaced or misconceived may be its understanding of the true object of its thirst.

CHAPTER 6

Christ Lifted Up

The Reproaches, like the gospels themselves, refer to, but do not describe, the act of crucifixion. No description was needed because it was a sight sadly familiar to the people of that time. Matthew merely alluded to the soldiers' action in crucifying Jesus in a subordinate clause, 'And when they had crucified him, they divided his clothes among themselves ...' (Mt 27:35). The Reproaches twice state, 'You led your Saviour to the cross', and the last Reproach, the climax of them all, shows the cross as the 'lifting up' of Christ in all the varied senses of that phrase:

> I raised you to the height of majesty,
> But you have raised me high on a cross.

We find here a change of metaphor, because most of the previous Reproaches are based on the word 'down' or contain the idea of Christ being 'thrown down' in his sufferings for us. 'You brought your scourges down on me.' 'You struck me down and scourged me.' These words evoke a picture in which the forces of evil and hate tower over the figure of Christ who was bowed down to the ground as a helpless, uncomplaining victim beneath them. The same thought is found in Reproaches like, 'You handed me over to your high priests', 'You led me to Pilate's court'. Christ is depicted here as under the power of a scheming, vindictive priesthood and the political might of an autocratic governor who colluded, though unwillingly, with their plans.

Christ, in being 'struck down', shared the fate of Israel's enemies who were defeated when they opposed Israel's escape from Egypt and settlement in the promised land. In so far as the outworking of God's plan for the salvation of humanity involved suffering, Christ shared that suffering:

> For your sake I scourged your captors and first-born sons,
> but you brought your scourges down on me.

> For you I struck down the kings of Canaan,
> but you struck my head with a reed.

As we noted at the end of chapter 2, the traditional form of the Reproaches reminds us of the tragedy, pain and cruelty in the human story for which God takes responsibility and which he brings into his own experience through being identified with suffering humanity in Christ.

'Lifted up' in Shame and Glory

There is a change of metaphor in the last two Reproaches which speak of Christ being 'lifted up', but it is a continuation of the same idea because it is a very ambiguous and ironic kind of 'lifting up' which Christ experienced. He was raised 'high on a cross' by Roman soldiers as a spectacle to the world of a condemned felon, his alleged crime placarded above his head for all to see. The thought of Christ being lifted up is prominent in St John's Gospel among the New Testament writers, and John made skillful use of irony and double meaning to proclaim the mystery of Christ. To appreciate the depth and subtlety of his words it is necessary to emphasise both the sheer, sordid, earthly brutality of the crucifixion and the glorious victory over evil which the cross represents. John had a binocular vision of Christ's suffering which encompassed the full reality of his passion. We can see both aspects of the truth in a characteristic passage:

> Jesus answered them, 'The hour has come for the Son of Man to be glorified. Very truly, I tell you, unless a grain of wheat falls into the earth and dies, it remains just a single grain; but if it dies, it bears much fruit ... Now my soul is troubled. And what shall I say – 'Father, save me from this hour'? No. It is for this reason that I have come to this hour. Father glorify your name.' Then a voice came from heaven, 'I have glorified it, and I will glorify it again.' The crowd standing there heard it and said that it was thunder. Others said, 'An angel has spoken to him.' Jesus answered, 'This voice has come for your sake, not for mine. Now is the judgment of this world; now the ruler of this world will be driven out. And I, when I am lifted up from the earth, will draw all people to myself.' He said this to indicate the kind of death he was to die (Jn 12:23-24, 27-33).

This narrative is John's equivalent of the agony in the garden described in the other three gospels. It was written in the light of Christ's resurrection and of many years' meditation by the author on the significance of Christ's saving work. Jesus naturally shrank from the horror of crucifixion, as the first three gospels clearly show. For John the death of Jesus is his glorification, and his being lifted up on the cross is the exaltation and enthronement of the King of kings. By the cross God is glorified and 'the ruler of this world' (v. 31) is driven out of the realm which rightly belongs to God. It is still true that Christ's death was a sordid, brutal fact. Wicked people (representative of all of us) raised up God's Son on a torture stake as a humiliating spectacle before the world, but God made this evil deed a victory over evil. To human view Christ was lifted up on the cross in shame and pain. The deeper reality is that human sin and cosmic evil were exposed on the cross in all their horror, and overcome by Christ's suffering love.

The thought of the cross as a victory over the forces of evil is also found in St Paul's writings. The shame of the cross is something in which to glory (Gal 6:14). For Paul it is precisely through the shame, folly and weakness of the cross that God's power is known:

> For Jews demand signs and Greeks desire wisdom, but we proclaim Christ crucified, a stumbling block to Jews and foolishness to Gentiles ... For God's foolishness is wiser than human wisdom, and God's weakness is stronger than human strength (1 Cor 1:21-23, 25).

The Christ showered with ignominy as he suffered won a glorious victory as he unmasked and destroyed the world's sin on the cross:

> And when you were dead in trespasses and the uncircumcision of your flesh, God made you alive together with him, when he forgave us all our trespasses, erasing the record that stood against us with its legal demands. He set this aside, nailing it to the cross. He disarmed the rulers and authorities and made a public example of them, triumphing over them in it (Col 2:13-15).

The paradox in these words is quite breath-taking. Jesus was nailed to the cross and he hung there helpless, the passive victim of human sin. Yet Paul saw God in Jesus as nailing the record of our sins to the cross and in that way freeing us from sin's power. Jesus was exhibited to the world as a condemned felon, helpless and unable to move. Yet Paul described him as making a public example of the forces of evil and leading them 'as captives in his triumphal procession' (v. 15, New English Bible translation). When a Roman general won a notable victory he was given a 'triumph', a procession through the streets of Rome with his prisoners of war paraded before him. Outwardly there could be nothing less like a victorious general than a crucified man, but that is the daring image Paul used to show how Christ in his passion defeated evil.

The Attractive Power of the Cross

We can see the triumph of the cross and its defeat of evil in Christ's words, 'And I, when I am lifted up from the earth, will draw all people to myself' (Jn 12:32). Earlier, in answer to the hostile question, 'Who are you?' (Jn 8:25), he had said, 'When you have lifted up the Son of Man, then you will realise that I am he' (v. 28). Only through being raised on a cross as a result of Christ's encounter with human sin could his true nature become known, that he is God's only Son and saviour of the world. The double meaning of the words 'lifted up' served John well to convey both the shame and the glory of the cross, the sordid fact of an unjust, cruel death and the triumphant reality of a mighty act of salvation. From a human view-point Jesus suffered a degrading, agonising form of execution. In God's eyes his suffering and death were his exaltation as the victorious lamb of God who defeated the evil which bound the human race and who is enthroned at God's right hand as saviour king.

The defeat of evil meant that human beings were rescued from its slavery and given healing and new life. 'And just as Moses lifted up the serpent in the wilderness, so must the Son of Man be lifted up, that whoever believes in him may have eternal life' (Jn 3:14-15). These words of Jesus allude to an episode in the Israelites' desert wanderings when snakes attacked the people. At God's command, 'Moses made a serpent of bronze, and put it upon a pole; and whenever a serpent bit someone, that person would look at the serpent of bronze and live' (Num 21:9). The representation of the cause of death became a means of healing and life. The supreme example of human sin, Christ's crucifixion, became the means of the world's salvation. In a similar way the crown of thorns, the mock sceptre and the satirical title, 'King of the Jews', bore unconscious witness to the true dignity of Christ the Saviour and the King of kings.

'And I, when I am lifted up from the earth, will draw all people to myself' (Jn 12:32). This process began even at the time of the crucifixion. Gathered round the cross were mockers and scoffers, the enemies of Jesus gloating over what they thought was the inglorious end of his career. But there were also present those who loved and mourned him. John stated that the mother of Jesus, Mary Magdalene, another Mary and the beloved disciple stood by the cross. Matthew and Mark, who emphasised most the desolation and rejection of Christ yet recorded that the centurion in charge of his execution was so moved by his death that he exclaimed, 'Truly this man was God's Son!' (Mk 15:39. See also Mt 27:54). Luke also noted the effect on the centurion who, 'praised God and said, "Certainly this man was innocent"' (Lk 23:47). Luke among the evangelists laid most stress on the reconciling effect of Christ's passion. Even before Jesus was condemned to death, Pilate and Herod made up their long-standing quarrel according to Luke, who clearly meant us to understand that this happened through their contact with Jesus (Lk 23:12). Luke recorded the conversion of the penitent robber who hung on the cross adjacent to that of Jesus (Lk 23:39-43). All four evangelists stated that Joseph of Arimathea performed the merciful task of giving Christ honourable burial and Matthew made the natural deduction that it was in his own tomb (Mt 27:60). John noted that the timid Nicodemus assisted Joseph in his task and provided a lavish amount of spices to wrap up with the body (Jn 19:39-40). The man who would only come to Jesus under cover of darkness during his lifetime was emboldened by Christ's death to be seen caring for his lifeless body in the light of day. Other evangelists mention the women who prepared spices for the grave (Mk 16:1; Lk 23:56). While it is difficult to harmonise all the accounts and to know the precise details of what happened, it is clear that a number of those associated with Jesus showed their respect for his dead body and came fully to believe in him after his resurrection.

Christ lifted up on the cross drew all these people to himself, deepening the love and faith of those who were already his disciples and awakening faith in some who were not. What Christ began in his passion he continues to do as long as his death is proclaimed. The effects of his passion are not confined to any age, group or time but are universal in their scope. 'I will draw *all* people to myself.' Christ died for the whole human race and his death has the power to bring everyone to God. St Cyril of Jerusalem said, 'On the cross, God stretched out his hands to embrace the ends of the earth,' and Jürgen Moltmann commented on his words that Christ hanging on the cross is the 'out-stretched God of the Trinity' (*The Crucified God* , p 207). Modern eucharistic rites contain similar words, as in the Church of England *Alternative Service Book*, 'He opened wide his arms for us on the cross'. It is not only that he invites or appeals to all to come; his death draws us like a magnet to God. Because of human freedom it is possible (at least theoretically) that some may finally and irrevocably reject the love and forgiveness which are so powerfully and at such great cost at work in the passion and death of Christ. But it is not God's will that any should be finally lost.

The Crucifixion and the Ascension

The words 'lifted up' refer primarily to the crucifixion. The evangelist commented, 'He said this to indicate the kind of death he was to die' (Jn 12:33). A victim on a cross was raised up a few feet higher than those standing on the ground, but the phrase 'lifted up from the earth' could not fail to remind readers of Christ's ascension into heaven. Earlier John had stated:

> No one has ascended into heaven except the one who descended from heaven, the Son of Man. And just as Moses lifted up the serpent in the wilderness so must the Son of Man be lifted up, that whoever believes in him may not perish but may have eternal life (Jn 3:13-15).

John deliberately used the expression 'lifted up' to describe both the crucifixion and the ascension. Luke also employs the phrase with this double sense, 'When the days drew near for him to be taken up, he set his face to go to Jerusalem' (Lk 9:51). Though we celebrate Good Friday and Ascension Thursday separately, and the two days have very different moods, they both proclaim the same truth, that the Christ raised up on the cross is raised up in glory to reign at God's right hand over the creation which he has redeemed by his suffering. The resurrection and ascension did not reverse the crucifixion; they revealed its deeper reality. John described Christ's death as 'going to the Father' (Jn 13:1, 16:28).

His crucifixion is a sort of ascension. While the death of Christ is the key event in his work of salvation, the New Testament writers never isolate his death from his rising again and ascending in heaven. He 'was handed over to death for our trespasses and was raised for our justification' (Rom 4:25). Christ is the Saviour 'who died, yes, who was raised, who is at the right hand of God, who indeed intercedes for us' (Rom 8:34).

Christ's atoning work consists of his life, death, resurrection and presence for us with God. The epistle to the Hebrews which interprets the salvation Christ achieved in terms of sacrifice, emphasises Christ's entry to the heavenly sanctuary 'now to appear in the presence of God on our behalf' (Heb 9:24). In the sacrificial ritual of the Old Testament, the animals were slaughtered in the outer courts of the temple and the priests brought the blood which was shed into the holy place. On the day of atonement each year the high priest brought the blood of the sacrificial animals into the holy of holies. The author of Hebrews used this practice to describe Christ's atoning work. Christ was crucified outside the holy city and he entered the holy of holies which is heaven itself where his sacrificial blood is all-sufficient atonement for the world's sins. 'He entered once for all into the Holy Place, not with the blood of goats and calves, but with his own blood, thus obtaining eternal redemption' (Heb 9:12).

The once for all sacrifice of Christ consists of his life on earth, his death on the cross, his resurrection and ascension and his perpetual appearance and intercession for us at God's right hand. This single, all-sufficient sacrifice is the means by which sinful people are brought back to God in every age and place. 'But when Christ had offered for all time a single sacrifice for sins, "he sat down at the right hand of God", and since then has been waiting "until his enemies would be made a footstool for his feet"' (Heb 10:12-13). The Christ who was 'lifted up from the earth' on to the cross as a sacrifice for sin was 'lifted up' by God to the throne of heaven where his once for all sacrifice is eternally effective because, by his perpetual intercession, he draws all people to himself and to his Father. The gospel of John and the epistle to the Hebrews combine to proclaim the exaltation of Jesus, on the cross and in heaven, as the salvation of the world.

Lifted up with Christ

> I raised you to the height of majesty,
> but you raised me high on a cross.

The result of Christ's exaltation on the cross and in heaven is that all who believe in him receive the fruits of his victory. The Reproach highlights the suffering inflicted on Christ when he was lifted up on the cross and contrasts it with God's gracious treatment of his people. No doubt the main reference is to God's rescue of Israel from Egypt and the high dignity he gave them as a free people, 'a kingdom of priests and a holy nation' (Ex 19:6). The 'reproach' is that God's own people, whom he treated so well, treated his Son so badly. But we can find a much fuller truth in the words. The liberation of God's ancient people from Egyptian slavery is a pointer to the much greater liberation God effected through Christ. Peter used the words of Exodus just quoted to describe God's renewed people who were freed by Christ's sacrifice and made a 'royal priesthood, a holy nation' (1 Pet 2:9). As we all deserve the reproach, so we can all share in the victory. God raised us 'to the height of majesty' through the fact that we raised Christ on a cross and were brought to reject the sins which crucified him. Christ died for us when we were sinful and his enemies. By absorbing in his own person the poison of our sin, he changed us from being his enemies to being his friends. 'For if while we were enemies, we were reconciled to God through the death of his son, much more surely, having been reconciled, will we be saved by his life' (Rom 5:10). Christ came where we are so that we might be where he is. He took our place of separation from God in order that he might bring us to his place of union with God. 'For you know the generous act of our Lord Jesus Christ, that though he was rich, yet for your sakes he became poor, so that by his poverty you might become rich' (2 Cor 8:9). By a 'wondrous exchange' the goodness of Christ replaces our wickedness, the obedience of Christ takes away our disobedience. This can only happen by a costly act of suffering and death. Christ performed that act and paid that price with the result that we can receive the riches of communion with God.

The New Testament has lavish promises to God's people of being raised with Christ and given a place on his heavenly throne. Christ said to his apostles:

> You are those who have stood by me in my trials; and I confer on you, just as my Father has conferred on me, a kingdom, so that you may eat and drink at my table in my kingdom, and you will sit on thrones judging the twelve tribes of Israel (Lk 22:28-30).

Their royal dignity is not to be confused with the pride and pomp of earthly dominion. A few verses earlier Jesus had rebuked his disciples for an untimely dispute about which of them was the greatest (vv. 24-27). He said that the kings of the Gentiles lord it over their subjects but it is to be 'not so with you'. The kingship they will exercise will be one of mutual service. It is no less a kingship for that; in fact, it is the only kind of royal power that will endure.

It is not only the apostles who share in Christ's kingship. The twelve apostles were the nucleus of the church and the promise of reigning with Christ extends to all whom Christ redeemed by his sacrificial death and who believe in him.

> For you were slaughtered and by your blood you ransomed for God saints from every tribe and language and people and nation; you have made them to be a kingdom and priests serving our God, and they will reign on earth (Rev 5:9-10).

St Paul in his letters frequently alluded to Christians sharing Christ's kingly state, sometimes to recall them from behaviour unworthy of their status. He rebuked the Corinthians for going to law with their fellow Christians before heathen magistrates by saying, 'Do you not know that we are to judge angels?' (1 Cor 6:3). He often used phrases like 'raised with Christ' (Col 3:1) and 'made us sit with him in the heavenly places' (Eph 2:6). Both Christ's death and glorification are meant to be experienced by his followers. 'We have been buried with him by baptism into death, so that, just as Christ was raised from the dead by the glory of the Father, so we too might walk in newness of life' (Rom 6:4).

> If we have died with him, we will also live with him;
> If we endure, we will also reign with him (2 Tim 2:11).

St John saw the death of Christ as itself his glorification, and the Christian too finds in the trials of being a disciple on earth something of the radiance of eternal glory. Stephen's face during his trial shone 'like the face of an angel' (Acts 6:15). Peter's martyrdom was described as 'the kind of death by which he would glorify God' (Jn 21:19). John's use of the phrase 'lifted up' with a double meaning refers not only to Christ but to Christ's followers who experience his victory when they bravely face persecution for their faith.

Our sharing in the exaltation of Christ is not merely an individual experience but is essentially something a body of people find in their life and worship together. Modern readers often fail to notice how much the Bible speaks of God's people, not as meaning the plural of 'individual', a collection of men and women, but as an organic whole. The sentence, 'They shall be my people and I will be their God', occurs (with minor variations) in many verses of the Old Testament, particularly in the prophets Jeremiah and Ezekiel, and is quoted in the New where it is applied to the church. The children of Israel were very definitely one people, by God's action. The sense of the nation having a single corporate life is so strong in many parts of the Old Testament that the individual appears to be lost, and books like Ezekiel correct the balance by teaching individual responsibility. The value of each person is clearly seen in the ministry of Christ and the life of the early church, but equally clearly the New Testament shows our membership of each other in Christ's body, God's people and God's family. Christians are united with Christ and each other as branches in a vine (Jn 15). Individual gifts are for the benefit of the whole body (1 Cor 12). 'We do not live to ourselves, and we do not die to ourselves' (Rom 14:7). Each Christian is to be a 'living stone' built into a 'spiritual house' (1Pet 2:4). It is the corporate body of Christians which inherits the promises of God fulfilled in Christ who makes us one people by his cross. He died 'to gather into one the dispersed children of God' (Jn 11:52). We are each most truly ourselves when we are not isolated individuals but persons in community. Sharing in Christ's kingship essentially belongs to the common life of those whom God has united in Christ. As the sin of the world raised up Christ on the cross, so we are raised to 'the height of majesty' as we receive forgiveness in a forgiven community.

Throughout history the Christian Church has often lost sight of its calling to live a life 'hidden with Christ in God' (Col 3:3) and become a pressure group or politically powerful institution seeking wealth and prestige in the world. Even at its best it is still a human organisation with all the imperfections and weaknesses that entails, as the pages of the New Testament plainly show. Yet it bears witness to a divine treasure in an earthly vessel and reminds the world of God's promises to humanity which include, but go beyond, the span of human life on earth. The Christian community views the problems of the world in which it is set in the light of the eternal value God places on his human family. Christians believe that the problems of this world cannot be solved by the resources of this world alone but that an eternal dimension is necessary to rescue humankind from its predicament. God's promise of abundant life, available on this earth but reaching out beyond the temporal scene, is the only lasting satisfaction for human need.

Christ proclaimed the kingdom of God on earth and achieved its dawning through his death and resurrection. What he has done releases us to the glory, pain and adventure of being fully alive – to God, to our fellow human beings and to the created world which we can either exploit and destroy or use with respect and wonder at its endless possibilities. The vision of human life which the gospel sets before us, as God's gift offered to mankind, is one of joy, harmony, creative activity, rest without boredom, exhilarating tasks and self-acceptance without pride. Christ's parables show us this gift of abundant life in terms of a wedding feast, a bountiful harvest in spite of weeds and stony ground, faithful use of resources (parable of the talents), sharing food with the hungry, forgiving wrongs and being forgiven. The anguish of the cross was necessary to bring in the kingdom and before its full coming a bitter struggle with evil remains, but Christ has won the decisive battle and those who believe in him share in his victory though they still have to suffer the pains of continuing conflict with all that is against God's will, both in themselves and in the world around them.

The company of Christ's followers is the first fruits of the kingdom and they are a pilgrim people charged to remind the world of the gift God has prepared for the whole human race. God gave his ancient people 'a royal sceptre' and raised them to 'height of majesty', as the Reproaches state. These are the gifts he offers all humanity through the work of Christ, accomplished once for all on the cross and continued both by his heavenly intercession and presence with his church on earth. The one who makes all things new (Rev 21:5) is bringing in his kingdom through those who acknowledge him and proclaim his promises to the world.

Praying for All

The whole world and its overwhelming needs have a prominent place in the traditional intercessions of the Good Friday liturgy. As the Reproaches show us what the human race has done to the Son of God, we go on to pray for all humanity for which he died. Past forms of these intercessions contained statements offensive to the Jewish people, as they blamed them exclusively in a quite unjustifiable way for the death of Christ. Modern liturgies have either omitted altogether special mention of the Jews in praying for all people, or included prayers which express the common responsibility of all of us, Jew and Gentile alike, for the sin which brought Jesus to the cross. For example, the Church of England *Lent, Holy Week, Easter* has the petition:

> Lord God of Abraham,
> bless the children of your covenant, both Jew and Christian;
> take from us all blindness and bitterness of heart,
> and hasten the coming of your kingdom,
> when Israel shall be saved,
> the Gentiles gathered in,
> and we shall dwell together in mutual love and peace under the one God and Father of our Lord Jesus Christ.

The cross is the last place where anyone can be judgemental about anyone else. Christ bore the sins of the world and we all need his forgiveness. It is appropriate on the day when we specially remember Christ's death that we intercede for all our fellow-sinners. The main petition must be that all members of the human family may know and respond to the good news of God's forgiveness offered at such great cost in Christ's passion and death, but God's love embraces all people whether they respond to it or not and the church's prayer is for the welfare of all. The Good Friday intercessions contain a large number of 'secular' concerns. There was nothing holy to outward view in the brutal, degrading death by torture which is crucifixion. The only religion shown there was religious hate, when the enemies of Jesus gloated over his sufferings. The hill outside Jerusalem where Jesus was executed beside two other condemned men was the scene where the worlds of politics, economics, vested interests, conflicting rights and issues of justice came together. This complex, ambiguous world marked by human sin, weakness and fear, is the world God loves and for which Christ died. Hence the church intercedes on Good Friday for all human life in its varied manifestations. We pray for the church itself, in the world and stained by the world's sin, that it may be faithful to the crucified one, remembering that religious people asked for Christ's death. Prayer is made for rulers and institutions of government, recognising the temptations of power and the perplexing decisions that have to be made in the conduct of human affairs. It is easy to condemn the vacillating and self-interested behaviour of Pilate in the trial of Christ and right to do so, but often in political life the issues are so complex that the just course of action is by no means clear. Our prayer for politicians in their human frailty can have no justification for self-righteousness, for it is something we all share.

Christ on the cross is identified with those on the edges of human society, life's failures, victims of personal and corporate sin, prisoners both innocent and guilty. An important place in the Good Friday intercessions is given to the oppressed, the persecuted, those discriminated against, the handicapped, the sick and the dying. Prayer is made also for those in doubt and despair, those who do not or cannot believe in God and those who struggle under the burden of severe temptation. Most difficult of all is prayer for those who inflict suffering, the oppressors and persecutors. The Solemn Intercession in the Canadian *Book of Alternative Services* has prayers 'for all who are enemies of the cross of Christ, and persecutors of his disciples, for all who in the name of Christ have persecuted others'. The Christ who taught us to love our enemies set us the most costly example imaginable when he prayed on the cross, 'Father, forgive them; for they do not know what they are doing' (Lk 23:34).

CHAPTER 7

The Reproaches and the Atonement

The great value of the Reproaches is that they present us with the fact of Christ's death on the cross, not simply as a truth to be accepted by the mind, but as an awareness with our whole being of God's amazing love for his sinful human family. How Christ's suffering and death effect the forgiveness of our sins will probably always be a mystery to human thought, and no explanation of the 'how' is an obligatory part of Christian belief. Yet we naturally wonder and try to puzzle out why Christ's death was necessary and how it frees us from the burden of sin. We are not trying to solve a problem for the mind in a purely intellectual way. Rather, our wish is to make sense of the human predicament as it is shared by Christ and the way Christ's sharing in it brings us release from evil's power. We are looking for something to speak to mind, heart and imagination so that we may know in the depths of our being, even if we cannot fully put the knowledge into words, the work of Christ which restores us to freedom, peace and new life. The Reproaches appeal to feeling as well as thought; they urge a response from the will to the great love of God demonstrated in Christ's cross. They encourage us to think about what Christ has done for us in a way which demands a change in outlook and behaviour. More than thought is needed, but thought must be included in our response to the crucified Christ.

The Cross as Moral Example

Among the traditional ways of looking at the atonement, the exemplary or moral influence theory taught by Abelard and others would naturally come first to mind when we hear the Reproaches. They show what our sins have done to God and his great love which went to such lengths to draw us to himself:

> I led you out of Egypt, from slavery to freedom,
> but you led your Saviour to the cross ...

I gave you a royal sceptre,
but you gave me a crown of thorns.

The appalling horror of human sin is plainly shown in the Reproaches. The God who made us and cares for us and came among us in the person of Christ is the one whom we human beings rejected and nailed to the cross. Christ's suffering is what our sin does to God. The cross demonstrates the abominable nature of sin and the Reproaches bring it home to us by listing the pains and humiliations Christ suffered during his passion. In order to be freed from sin we need to be faced with its horror. Sometimes the sufferings of Christ are preached to us in ways which produce morbid and neurotic self-hate and an inappropriate sense of personal guilt for what happened to Christ. But we can reject this distortion of the truth and also see the genuine insight which lies behind it, that the wrong we do is an injury to God.

God's love, demonstrated in Christ's cross, quickly leads us from revulsion at our sins which caused his passion to gratitude for what he has done and the desire to live by the moral ideal of sacrificial love. The emotional impact of the Reproaches is similar to that of Isaac Watts' lines,

Love so amazing, so divine
demands my soul, my life, my all.

Christ hanging on the cross has inspired countless people in every age, not all of them members of his church, to follow the way of non-violence and overcome evil with good. Isaac Watts' hymn quoted above was a favourite of Mahatma Gandhi. Christ's example of love for his enemies, as shown by his prayer for them on the cross, was followed by Stephen, the first Christian martyr, as he was being stoned to death when he prayed in similar words, 'Lord, do not hold this sin against them' (Acts 7:60). The New Testament writers explicitly quote Christ's example when appealing to Christians to return kindness for cruelty, love for hate. 'For to this you have been called, because Christ also suffered for you, leaving you an example, so that you should follow in his steps … When he was abused, he did not return abuse; when he suffered, he did not threaten; but he entrusted himself to the one who judges justly' (1 Pet 2:21, 23).

The Victory of the Cross

The cross is not merely an appeal to heart and mind to forsake evil and turn to God. It is not just a demonstration of God's love; it is that love in action, conquering evil, paying the ransom price which frees us from evil's power, cancelling God's righteous condemnation of sinners. These are different metaphors which attempt to express a many-sided truth. The thought of the cross as a victory over evil has a firm basis in the New Testament, is prominent in the early church fathers and was given wide currency in this century by the Swedish theologian Gustaf Aulén through his book *Christus Victor* (1931). It is not explicit in the main body of the Reproaches though, as we noted in the previous chapter, it is implied in the phrase 'lifted up' when viewed against its usage by John and Paul. The note of victory is clearly heard in the response, 'Holy is God! Holy and strong! Holy immortal one, have mercy on us', and even more strongly in the hymn, 'Sing my tongue the glorious battle'.

The exemplary theory of the atonement contains hints of the cross as a victory of love over hate, though by itself it does not go far enough in showing Christ's sufferings as God's mighty act of salvation. How can the agonising, shameful death which Christ suffered be regarded as a victory over evil? To understand something of the victory of the cross it is necessary to look at the nature of the enemy which is defeated. The essence of evil lies in the will, the choosing of what is wrong. It is not simply a case of individuals choosing separately to do wrong, but there is a corporate dimension to sin which affects the human race as a whole. Human beings can be so enslaved to evil habits that there is virtually no choice in their continuing to do evil, and the corporate wickedness of humanity is a further enslavement. But though our power of choice is greatly restricted, yet the interaction of individuals with society and the choices made in one person's life over a period of time, mean that the human will is the scene, the only arena where evil can get a foothold in humanity. To conquer evil is to deal with the human will.

Force is not enough to root out evil from our wills. At most force can restrain evil and prevent its worst effects. Every country needs a system of policing to protect its citizens from the wrongdoing of its lawless elements. Severe punishments for offenders and the strong possibility that they will be caught by an efficient and impartial police force may deter people from committing crime but cannot change their hearts. An omnipotent God could prevent human beings from doing anything wrong but that would not make us good. To root out evil from humanity it is necessary to effect a change in our inner nature so that we willingly, not out of fear or because we are coerced, turn from evil to God and allow him to empower us to do good. Even for God that is a task of the utmost difficulty because it does not require the exercise of superior force but depends on God's appeal to our hearts and wills. We can see how hard it is even for God to rescue us from evil by the agony and bloody sweat of Jesus in the garden of Gethsemane and his anguished cry on the cross, 'My God, my God, why have you forsaken me?' When he made a world of free human beings God limited himself, voluntarily restricted his ability to control everything by sheer might and allowed himself to be vulnerable to the wilfulness of humanity. The cost to him of winning the free response of human beings to his love was the cross of Christ.

The Good Friday Reproaches show God, not threatening the world with destruction or forcing people to do his will against their own will, but pleading with them on the basis of Christ's sufferings. God, without any worries about his own dignity, argues, appeals, does everything possible to break through the shell of indifference, fear, weakness, obstinacy and pride which the corporate sin of the human race has put in place to shield us from God's love. The refrain to the Reproaches, 'Holy is God! Holy and strong, Holy immortal one, have mercy on us!', recognises the power of God's love, the power of suffering which is effective where the power of force can do nothing.

But it is not merely as an appeal to our hearts and minds that the victory of the cross is seen. It is not enough to be sorry for our sins, or even (if it were possible) to forsake sin in the future. Past sin must be taken away by a mighty act of God. 'Have you not yet considered what a heavy weight sin is?' (Anselm, *Cur Deus Homo?* XXI). The cross represents the concentrated power of all evil directed at the suffering Christ who patiently, with love for all humanity, absorbs its poison, is killed by it, and by his death deprives evil of its power. When Paul described how God in Christ forgave us our sins and erased 'the record that stood against us with its legal demands', he went on to say, 'He disarmed the rulers and authorities and made a public example of them, triumphing over them in it' (Col 2:13-15). Much of the New Testament speaks of the conflict between good and evil. Christ saw his ministry as a contest with Satan from the time of his temptations in the wilderness to his crucifixion. When he healed the sick he was undoing the work of the evil one, casting out devils. He regarded Peter's well-meant attempt to dissuade him from following the way of the cross as the voice of Satan (Mk 8:33). John represented Jesus as saying that his being 'lifted up' caused the expulsion of Satan from this world (Jn 12:31-32). Revelation, the last book of the New Testament, is full of the theme that the hosts of Satan have been conquered by 'the blood of the Lamb' (Rev 12:11).

Behind this way of speaking lies a picture of cosmic evil as a mighty host of wicked supernatural beings, under their great captain Satan, who hold the universe in thrall. Christ did battle with this mighty enemy to rescue all creation from its power. The lonely figure on the cross appeared to be the defeated victim of the devil and his servants but in reality Christ has given evil its death wound. Christ really suffered and died but by doing so he conquered death and freed humanity from the dominion of sin. He became the target for the concentrated force of all evil. The innocent victim of the world's sin absorbed its poison in his own person, was killed by it and by his death deprived evil of its power. Christ the sinless one so identified himself with sinful humanity that he was killed by the burden of sin, but his death rescued us from sin's dominion. That is the victory of the cross.

To speak of a mighty war between supernatural armies may sound incredible or meaningless to many moderns, yet the horrors of this century show evil on such a colossal scale that our ordinary words to describe it seem woefully inadequate. Scientific advance, which has done so much for human welfare, has also made possible refinements of cruelty and destructive capability undreamt of in earlier centuries, to the extent that all life on earth is in danger from nuclear bombs or pollution of land and sea. Living under such threats gives more meaning to the language of cosmic battle than would appeal to people in calmer, safer ages. Stories of titanic struggle between good and evil, through their powerful imagery, may convey more to our end of millenium fears than the down to earth language of literal prose.

The Cross as Ransom

The idea of ransom is closely connected with that of victory as an attempt to show how Christ's death frees us from our sins. In the days when prisoners of war were sold into slavery unless their friends could raise the money to buy their freedom, the thought of ransom to describe Christ's saving work would mean a lot to the first hearers of the gospel. Christ said, 'For the Son of Man came not to be served but to serve, and to give his life a ransom for many' (Mk 10:45). The human race by its collective sin has been sold into slavery and only God, through Christ's death, can pay the price of our freedom.

The New Testament nowhere develops the metaphor of ransom to the extent of asking to whom the ransom is paid, but this question exercised many later Christian thinkers. Some of the fathers taught that the ransom was paid to the devil, but that he could not hold on to the prize he had gained in the death of Christ because Christ rose from the dead. Gregory of Nyssa elaborated the metaphor to bizarre lengths:

> Since the hostile power was not going to enter into relations with a God present unveiled, or endure His appearance in heavenly glory, therefore God, in order to render Himself accessible to him who demanded of Him a ransom for us, concealed Himself under the veil of our nature, in order that, as happens with greedy fishes, together with the bait of the flesh the hook of the Godhead might also be swallowed, and so, through Life passing over into death, and the Light arising in the darkness, that which is opposed to Life and Light might be brought to nought. For darkness cannot endure when the Light shines, nor can death remain in being where Life is active (quoted by Aulén, *Christus Victor*, p 68).

Can we find any insight of value into the atonement behind this grotesque picture? The idea of ransom adds a new thought to the victory concept of Christ's death. The evil which Christ defeated on the cross is not simply an external calamity visited on innocent people. We human beings have listened to the devil's temptations and must take our share of the blame. The tragic hero in literature usually has some fatal moral weakness which his enemies can exploit to bring about his inevitable downfall. Christ's victory over evil is not a straightforward battle against an external foe to rescue blameless prisoners but takes into account our connivance with the devil's wiles. We have sold ourselves into the devil's hands, making a very bad bargain, it is true, but with some responsibility for the tragic result. It is in a sense right and just that we are Satan's prisoners and our rescue must be in accordance with justice. This seems to be the insight behind the idea of Christ's death as a ransom paid to the devil. The scenario is reminiscent of a frequent theme in Victorian novels, a young man falls into dissipation, debt and the clutches of an unscrupulous money-lender. He signs bill after bill for ready cash until he is enmeshed in a net from which he cannot get free. Then his father comes to the rescue, pays the debt in full and gives his son a fresh start. For complete poetic justice the rascally money-lender should be exposed and punished as well (and that perhaps is the valid insight in the idea that Christ outwitted the devil), but the debts the young man has incurred need to be paid.

Christ the Sin-bearer

The Reproaches do not contain any thought of Christ's victory as a ransom paid but they implicitly convey the related idea that Christ bore the sufferings which were our due. In a series of striking contrasts, God's loving treatment of his people is compared with the pains Christ endured. The immediate impact of the Reproaches is to awaken our consciences to what we have done to God by our sins and bring us to repent, but further reflection leads us to see that forgiveness of our sins involves Christ taking our place as the victim of sin. 'I gave you a royal sceptre, but you gave me a crown of thorns.' 'I raised you to the height of majesty, but you have raised me high on a cross.' As we noted in the previous chapter, our royal sceptre was only possible through Christ wearing the crown of thorns and our enthronement with Christ cost his elevation on the cross of suffering and shame. We escaped the terrible consequences of our sins because Christ endured them instead. The contrasts of the Reproaches imply that Christ is in some sense our substitute. We have all the benefits; Christ suffered all the agony, pain and loss. God in Christ bore the cost of our sins, as the king in the parable of the unmerciful servant bore the loss of the ten thousand talents that the servant could not pay (Mt 18:23-35).

It is sometimes said that Christ bore the punishment due to all humanity for their sins. The holy and righteous God cannot simply overlook wrong doing, he must for the sake of justice exact a penalty. The wrath of God against sinners fell on Christ, the sinless one who bore it patiently and in that way brought it to an end. If we are to find any insight of value in this way of speaking we must reject outright those forms of it which are morally repulsive and unworthy of the God revealed in Christ. The idea must be rejected that there is any unwillingness on God's part to forgive or that the punishment of Christ is a prior condition of God's forgiveness. Such a view divides Christ's will from God's and makes Christ more forgiving than God. 'In Christ God was reconciling the world to himself, not counting their trespasses against them' (2 Cor 5:19). The atonement was from beginning to end the work of God, not that Christ alone made atonement and God the Father then forgave us. The Reproaches, like the Bible, show the Father and the Son at one in the work of the world's salvation. The personal pronoun 'I' can only be taken as referring to Father and Son together. 'I planted you as my fairest vine ... when I was thirsty you gave me vinegar to drink'.

It is at best highly misleading to say that Christ suffered punishment to appease God's wrath. A good person must feel anger against wrong doing. There are circumstances where it would be wrong not to feel angry. If we believe that God is good, there must be something in him corresponding to human indignation against sin, without the defects which accompany any human emotion. The Reproaches follow the Bible in showing a passionate God who cares deeply about his human family, and their biblical language of love, pleading and condemnation can speak to us more deeply than the abstract terms sometimes used. The wrath of God against sin must be dealt with in the process of forgiveness, but it is monstrous to assert that God's anger against the guilty is appeased by his punishment of the innocent. Such a course would increase righteous anger, not reduce or take it away. A bad-tempered man will lash out at the nearest victim whether guilty or not and can often in that way get rid of his anger, but it would be blasphemous to regard God's indignation against sin in any such terms. Whatever is meant by dealing with God's righteous anger against sin, it cannot be that. Both God and Christ are angry at sin. The gospels frankly record the times when Jesus was angry. God and Christ together deal with divine wrath against evil. 'The expiation is made in the heart and life of God himself' (D. M. Baillie, *God was in Christ*, p 178).

Having cleared the ground of these misunderstandings, we can now look for the genuine insights in language of Christ bearing the penalty of our sins. Perhaps the question is best approached by looking at what is involved in forgiveness. It is sometimes assumed that when we forgive someone we make light of their sins. This is a surprising mistake because when we make light of the offence we do not really forgive. 'It doesn't matter.' 'There is nothing to forgive.' Expressions like these recognise that there is no forgiveness unless we fully face up to the wrong done. When we really forgive those who wrong us, we deal with the wrong in all its seriousness. That is the only kind of forgiveness which is worth anything and it is costly and painful. We can dimly see that God's act of forgiving the sins of the world was at a price beyond human imagining. The cross is the measure of the cost.

The better the person the more ready he is to forgive and the more his forgiveness will cost him. Suppose a son brings terrible disgrace on a family. A father who cares little or nothing about his son's behaviour will not mind unduly, but one whose own conduct is consistently good will feel keenly the wrongness of what his son has done and will share in the disgrace. Suppose also that the father does not cast off his son, does not protect his own reputation by forbidding him the house and ending all communication with him, but lets him know that he will welcome him home, pay his debts, face the hostility of those he has wronged, and still love him as a son, in no way condoning his sin but receiving him into the family. That is costly and true forgiveness.

No two human beings are as close to each other as Christ is to sinful humanity. The human father shares his son's disgrace to some extent and the better he is the more he will grieve over the evil itself rather than the loss to his reputation. Yet people will not judge him as severely as they will his son, and he cannot regard his son's wrongdoing as totally his own. But in the case of Christ his identification with a sinful human race was complete. Nobody is an isolated individual. What we are is determined by our relationships with each other, both in our goodness and our sin. Our membership one of another in the body of Christ is the redemption of our destructive solidarity through bondage to one another in a sinful state. Christ, the sinless one, entered fully into this destructive network and became both its victim and its redeemer. He was 'numbered with the transgressors', he was condemned to death as a criminal and executed alongside wicked men. Out of his great love for us he became totally at one with us in the separation from God which sin inevitably brings, in God's just condemnation of sin, in order that he might share with us his goodness and nearness to God. He wore the crown of thorns that rightly belongs to us in order to give us a royal sceptre. 'For our sake [God] made him to be sin who knew no sin, so that in him we might become the righteousness of God' (2 Cor 5:21).

Another way to see the need for costly atonement as part of true forgiveness is to think of a terrible wrong done against a defenceless, innocent victim. Not only is it hard to forgive, one wonders if it is even right to forgive such an act. If forgiveness is to be genuine, something has to be done to make restitution where that is possible and at least to recognise fully the depth of the wrong. If an adult cruelly ill-treats a child he should not be forgiven (indeed cannot be forgiven) unless he is made to regard his actions with horror and disgust. Where it is possible to help the child recover from his physical and psychological wounds, the offender should contribute what he can to the cost. Our moral sense demands that he serve a time in prison, its length proportionate to the seriousness of his crime. The object of any punishment he undergoes is to satisfy justice and to bring him to repentance. Retribution against wrong should not be separated from efforts to reform the wrongdoer. Our indignation against evil becomes distorted if we simply demand the utmost vengeance without even the wish that the offender should repent. It is possible to be so consumed with hate for evil that we are disappointed by signs of repentance and prefer that the one sinning should remain evil so that we can indulge the luxury of hating him. In such a case we have become infected with the evil and we also need to repent. But this distortion of moral indignation does not negate the rightness of an appropriate anger against the sort of behaviour we have described, and therefore against all wrongdoing. It is this proper sense of moral outrage that must be dealt with in true forgiveness.

Probably nowhere in literature has the problem of sin and forgiveness been so forcefully stated as in Dostoyevsky's novel *The Brothers Karamazov* in the famous argument between Ivan and his brother the novice monk Alyosha. Ivan gave the instance of the general who owned an estate with a thousand serfs and the child of one of them, a boy of eight, threw a stone which hurt the paw of his favourite hound. The general in his rage set the whole pack of borzoi hounds on the child, in the sight of his mother, and they tore him to pieces. Ivan then challenged Alyosha with the enormity of this evil and how nothing can put it right. He exclaimed,

> And, finally, I do not want a mother to embrace the torturer who had her child torn to pieces by his dogs! She has no right to forgive him! If she likes, she can forgive him for herself, she can forgive the torturer for the immeasurable suffering he has inflicted upon her as a mother; but she has no right to forgive him for the sufferings of her tortured child. She has no right to forgive the torturer for that, even if her child were to forgive him! And if that is so, if they have no right to forgive, what becomes of the harmony? Is there in the whole world a being who could or would have the right to forgive? I don't want harmony. I don't want it, out of the love I bear to mankind. I want to remain with my suffering unavenged and my indignation unappeased, *even if I were wrong* (Vol I, p 287).

We can feel intense sympathy with Ivan's outlook. Any answer to him which lessens the horror and monstrosity of such cruelty on a helpless child must be rejected out of hand. If forgiveness is possible it must be *right*, it must take full account of the enormity of the evil done. Ivan seems to reject any 'higher harmony' in which sin is expiated. But is his position of unending moral indignation, 'my indignation unappeased', a satisfactory stopping point? Do we simply want to go on hating the cruel general for ever?

Alyosha admitted that Ivan was right in his indignation but took up his question, 'is there a being in the whole world who could or had the right to forgive?' He replied, 'But there is such a being, and he can forgive everything, everyone and everything and *for everything*, because he gave his innocent blood for all and for everything.' Ivan made no direct comment on Alyosha's answer so we cannot say if it satisfied him, but at least we can see that an answer is required and that it lies in the sacrifice of Christ even if we do not know exactly how.

Our sense of right and wrong requires that the torturer must come to see the horror of what he has done, must face up to the totally unjustified suffering he has caused. In the case of the Russian general he must come face to face with the mother of the child he has tortured to death, see the wrong he has done and realise that he cannot put it right. What is true of a particular sin is also true of all sin. Repentance, if it is to be real, requires not only such restitution as is possible but also the painful knowledge that the evil doer cannot undo the evil. Can anyone undo it? Does punishment cancel out crime? Can the sin of the guilty be expiated by the punishment of the innocent? We are concerned with real forgiveness which takes evil seriously and is in accordance with the moral order. It is immoral and unjust to punish the innocent for the sin of the guilty in any straightforward sense. A royal court in bygone days was said to have a whipping boy who was punished every time the young prince did wrong. Such a practice is morally repulsive and can have no connection with Christ suffering for our sins. Yet if Christ is to have 'the right to forgive' we can dimly see that he must absorb evil and this involves suffering. We look for the victory of good over evil, a real victory which deals with the horrible entail of evil though it can never change the fact that evil happened. Repentance is clearly a key element in the victory over evil, but the repentance of sinful people is never enough. They can never have a full sense of the wrongness of their sins, and even their partial awareness of it makes them realise that they cannot put it right, no matter how deep their penitence. Sinful people do wrong. Only a good person can realise the enormity of wrong. Christ, the sinless one, in solidarity with sinful human nature, is able to make atonement for the sum of human wrongdoing. 'The LORD has laid on him the iniquity of us all' (Isa 53:6). It is not that God punished Jesus for our sins. God, Father, Son and Holy Spirit, took on himself the responsibility for the human race he had created and given the dangerous gift of freedom. He bore the consequences of human misuse of freedom and that entailed the crucifixion. In Christ, God identified himself with sinful humanity, became one with them in their alienation from him, their God-forsakenness, in order to make them one with him as forgiven people. God 'in man, for man' performed a costly act of expiation which man could not do, in order to make the free gift of reconciliation which man can receive through repentance.

Language of punishment in connection with the atonement is

not particularly helpful and it is sometimes expressed in ways which make God both unloving and unjust. Yet behind such language there is the important insight that genuine forgiveness has to be just and right. In the centuries immediately before Christ's coming, the Jewish nation was severely persecuted and their sufferings may have prepared the ground for the Christian understanding of Christ's sufferings as having redemptive value. The older idea was that God meted out rewards and punishments according to human deserts; the bad suffered and the good prospered. But experience did not show an exact correspondence between virtue and earthly reward. Why did God allow the innocent to suffer? The conviction grew that their sufferings were not in vain. God had not forgotten them but would bring good out of their anguish. Somehow the guilt of the people as a whole could be taken away by suffering patiently borne, and this view was reinforced by a powerful sense of the corporate personality of the nation. The Suffering Servant songs in the second part of Isaiah represent God's righteous servant as willingly taking on the burden of the people's sins while being innocent himself.

> But he was wounded for our transgressions,
> crushed for our iniquities;
> upon him was the punishment that made us whole,
> and by his bruises we are healed.
> All we like sheep have gone astray;
> we have all turned to our own way,
> and the LORD has laid on him
> the iniquity of us all (Isa 53:5-6).

There was more severe persecution in the following centuries and under Greek rule strict Jews suffered appalling tortures for their faith, as described with horrifying detail in the books of the Maccabees. One of the martyrs prayed, 'Be merciful to your people, and let our punishment suffice for them. Make my blood their purification, and take my life in exchange for theirs' (4 Macc 6:28-29).

We can see in this way of thinking a strong awareness of solidarity with the nation and a great love for the whole people, to the extent that the martyrs are willing to take on themselves the suffering due to all because of the nation's sin. It would be false to the spirit of these writings to interpret them in strict legalistic and mechanical terms, as if one could put sin in one scale and corresponding suffering to balance it in the other. The Maccabean martyr's prayer shows his love for his people, his consciousness of the nation's sin and his offering of the extreme torture he endures to God for the people's sake, rather than a statement from God's side of what is necessary for their forgiveness. But underlying the passages from Isaiah and the books of the Maccabees is the conviction that a righteous loving God will save his people from their sins in a way which is both righteous and loving. That will inevitably be through suffering and not without suffering.

When we look at the cross of Christ we see God himself, in man and for man, doing what man could not do and bringing salvation to the human race. That implies both that Christ made atonement apart from us by taking our place and also that he incorporates us in his own communion with God. He died in our place in order to bring us to his place. In Tom Smail's words:

> What he did for us and without us on the cross has its whole goal in what he will do in us by joining us in union with himself by his Spirit, so that we are reconciled to God in him and are enabled to participate in his fulfilment of our covenant with God (*Atonement Today*, ed. J. Goldingay, p 91).

A full explanation of why the cross is necessary and how it brings salvation is not possible but the language of sin-bearing can communicate with our deep, inarticulate conviction that real forgiveness involves suffering. It is that conviction which we find in the Reproaches, in their contrasts between Christ's fate and the people's blessings:

> I raised you to the height of majesty,
> but you raised me high on a cross.

Christ the Liberator

The cross of Christ has always had a special appeal for the downtrodden and the oppressed. The poor and the deprived have felt a special affinity with the suffering Christ to whom they can turn with confidence, knowing that he shared their lot. The liberation theologian Jon Sobrino stated, 'Until today the Christ of the poor masses of Latin America is the suffering Christ, with the result that Holy Week is the most important religious occasion of the year, and within that Good Friday, and within that the laying of Christ in the tomb' (*Jesus the Liberator*, p

12). Human sin throughout history has often consisted of the exploitation of the weak by the strong, as we have come to realise more clearly in this century. Powerful nations have invaded, overrun and enslaved countries which could not resist them. At best, the subject nations saw much of their wealth go to their conquerors, though they may have benefited from some economic advance. At worst, they were exterminated, deported or reduced to slavery and their culture destroyed. Within nations, also, one class often dominated whole peoples, grabbing most of the country's wealth for itself and keeping the majority of the population in poverty and hunger. Many were exploited on the grounds of race, religion or language, when a dominant group used its power to deprive other sections of the community of their rights. The oppressed in many cases revolted against their oppressors and sometimes improved their lot, though it could happen that one set of oppressors simply took the place of another. Throughout history, women on the whole have suffered more oppression than men. Their subjection to men was often assumed, even by women themselves, to be natural and right. Oppression can occur even when a country's laws are reasonably fair and equitable because good laws have been subverted by bribery and corruption. As well as that, when a society is deeply divided and the memory of historic wrongs still rankles, when different groups are prejudiced and intolerant towards each other, then they will discriminate unfairly in giving employment, houses and opportunities to improve conditions of life. The whole catalogue of man's inhumanity to man is a clear sign that something is deeply wrong with human society and with individual human beings. Christ on the cross bore the burden of all this wrong and through the cross he sets us free from oppression, from the hate which tears communities apart and from the bitterness which poisons human lives.

The cross sets us free. How does this truth affect our understanding of the atonement? What light do the Reproaches throw on this aspect of Christ's saving work? Freedom is a prominent theme in the Reproaches. 'I led you out of Egypt, from slavery to freedom.' 'I scourged your captors...' 'I gave you a royal sceptre.' 'I raised you to the height of majesty.' The primary reference is to the freedom God gave the Israelite slaves from their Egyptian masters. Christ's passion is contrasted with the freedom, love and care God gave his people. But we argued in dealing with particular Reproaches that 'God's people' cannot be confined to Israel and that Christ's bearing the pain and shame of the cross was the means by which the whole of God's human family could receive freedom and new life. Christ is the one who sets the captives free, who breaks the oppressor's yoke, who defeats all that enslaves humanity. Human sin is the root of all oppression, and everyone, oppressor and oppressed alike, needs to be freed from its tyranny. Yet while the radical evil is the stranglehold of sin, freedom is not simply personal forgiveness, inner peace of mind and resignation under the rule of tyrannical masters. The liberation theologians of this century have shed new light on the Bible's concepts of salvation by drawing our attention to the social and political implications of God's action in Christ. Sometimes they overstate their case and we need not accept uncritically everything they say, but we need to be challenged by their Bible-based critique of social injustice with which the church has often colluded. God's gift of freedom in Christ is opposed to all that enslaves human beings and human communities. The gospel calls us to oppose in Christ's name every form of tyranny and to allign ourselves with the victims of tyranny in their struggles for justice. The emphasis on God's gift of freedom in the Reproaches encourages us to examine Christ's passion as a mighty act of liberation for the human race.

Christ frees us from the burden of sin and guilt, whatever the circumstances of our lives, so that we can be forgiven and find peace with God. The slave, the prisoner and the exploited do not have to wait for political liberation before they can experience new life in Christ. He was not the political Messiah many Jews expected, who would free Israel from Roman rule, but the one who rescues humanity from the tyranny of sin. Yet it is increasingly recognised that this is only part of the truth. While Christ did not found a political party or revolutionary movement dedicated to throw off foreign rule by force if necessary, he did proclaim a revolutionary message whose political implications the poor and the deprived are beginning to rediscover. Jesus proclaimed the kingdom of God and taught that children, the weak, the poor and those on the edges of society have a special welcome in the kingdom. He reinforced his words with his actions, the signs of the kingdom which he performed – healing the sick, casting out demons, feeding the hungry and dining with society's rejects. He taught his disciples to pray, 'Thy kingdom come, thy will be done, on earth as it is in heaven'. The kingdom is God's rule and since God is sovereign Lord over all creation his rule cannot be confined to personal and spiritual matters but must extend to every aspect of human life, including the way society is organised.

When Christ proclaimed and began to bring in the kingdom, he was fulfilling the Old Testament vision of God's rule. He claimed in his home synagogue of Nazareth that Isaiah's prophecy was fulfilled in him:

> The Spirit of the Lord is upon me,
> because he has anointed me to bring good news to the poor.
> He has sent me to proclaim release to the captives
> and recovery of sight to the blind,
> to let the oppressed go free,
> to proclaim the year of the Lord's favour
> (Lk 4:18-19. Isa 61:1-2).

The New Testament writers understood Jesus to embody God's just rule over the world. Paul paraphrased Isaiah's words:

> The root of Jesse shall come,
> the one who rises to rule the Gentiles;
> in him the Gentiles shall hope (Rom 15:12, Isa 11:10).

Throughout much of the Old Testament, we hear the cry of the oppressed to God and the promise that God will give them justice. Christ fulfilled God's promise, bringing hope to the world not simply of individual forgiveness and spiritual freedom but of the kingdom which begins God's just rule on earth. Hence he inevitably came into conflict with the anti-kingdom forces which brought him to the cross. Some nineteenth century liberal interpretations of Jesus, it is claimed, made him so innocuous a figure that it is hard to see why anyone would want to crucify him. Much of his ministry was marked by conflict with the rich, the powerful and the religious and political authorities of his day. It was not that he condemned them simply because of the class to which they belonged. He accepted invitations to dine with Pharisees and with the rich tax-collector, Zachaeus. He healed the servant of a Roman soldier, a member of his country's occupying forces, and praised his faith. But he denounced the oppressive way in which the authorities exercised power. He pointedly rejected the established political systems of his day when he said at the last supper, 'The kings of the Gentiles lord it over them; and those in authority over them are called benefactors. But not so with you; rather the greatest among you must become like the youngest, and the leader like one who serves' (Lk 22:25-26). His parables of the rich man and Lazarus (Lk 16:19-31) and the sheep and the goats (Mt 25:31-46) show how God takes the side of the downtrodden and condemns their oppressors and those who ignore their plight. His cleansing of the temple brought him into direct conflict with those who ran the temple, whom he called 'a den of robbers' (Mk 11:17). He clearly regarded the excessive charges which the worshippers had to pay as an exploitation of the poor.

Christ gave people a sense of their great value in God's sight, especially those who were nobodies in the eyes of the powerful and even possibly in their own eyes. He filled them with a sense of worth so that they could stand up with dignity, knowing that they had a share in the kingdom of God. This was immediate good news for them, unlike the purely political utopias which transfer the happy state to the future and fix the hopes of the downtrodden solely on the good time to come. Jesus taught that even when we are poor, weak, enslaved and hungry, we are blessed because of our present share in the kingdom as well as our hope for the future (Mt 5:3-12; Lk 6:20-23). But his words should not be interpreted as passive, resigned acceptance of slavery, poverty, injustice or oppression. Rather they give us a sense of our value to God which is ennobling, which frees us from a servile mentality and which gives us the incentive to strive for justice for all in ways that God approves of. Self-worth can be experienced even in states of slavery, unjust imprisonment and economic exploitation, but to acquiesce in such states is not to be fully alive. To suppress indignation against the oppressor is not true humility. To concentrate all our attention on the reversal of values in the next life, to make heaven a compensation for the injustices of earth, is to forget the revolutionary message of Christ's life.

It is not surprising that Christ's actions and words created a ferment in the Israel of his day which frightened the country's rulers. Jesus was more of a threat to the established order than Barabbas was (Sobrino, *Jesus the Liberator*, p 209). Barabbas probably belonged to the Zealot party and had been arrested in some minor skirmish with the Romans (Mk 15:7). Revolts such as the one he was involved in could be suppressed by force of arms, but Jesus was a more radical revolutionary because he went to the roots of what enslaved people and inspired them with a vision to transform human society more thoroughly than the replacement of one set of rulers by another. Jesus was accused at his trial of stirring up the people (Lk 23:5). The charge came from his opponents but was not necessarily false, as it seems likely that his teaching had disturbed the calm surface of the nation's life and aroused the expectation that God was about to act in a special way to establish justice. (It is important to remember that the leaders of the Sanhedrin supported the status quo in Israel as they feared a revolt would make the situation worse.) Any tyrannical regime would be anxious if something shook the mass of the people out of their apathy and made them eager for a change in their downtrodden state. Jesus was crucified as a troublemaker. The hope of new life in freedom which he gave inevitably led to his passion and death.

'Freedom' must be an element in our understanding of the atonement. The cross is God's great act of liberation of humanity, not only from the bonds of personal sin but also from the enslaving structures and the dehumanising effects of social evil. 'I led you from slavery to freedom but you led your Saviour to a cross.' 'I am the LORD your God who brought you out of the land of Egypt to be their slaves no more; I have broken the bars of your yoke and made you walk upright' (Lev 26:13). Christ gave us the true freedom of which the exodus from Egypt is a foretaste, precisely because he willingly accepted the status of a slave and suffered a slave's death. He identified himself with the enslaved when he was crucified between two bandits and he frees all slaves in his resurrection from the dead. Nietzsche was greatly mistaken when he described Christian ethics as a slave morality, though Christians through the centuries have often given credence to his view by misinterpreting meekness as putting up with oppression and by their collusion with the oppressors. It was not until the nineteenth century that the whole Christian Church woke up to the fact that slavery is wrong. All the more credit is due to people like Wilberforce who worked tirelessly to change centuries-old attitudes and to earlier pioneers such as the Society of Friends who led the way in freeing slaves. We can now see with hindsight that the New Testament contains a dynamic which condemns slavery and all other forms of oppression, even though its writings take this feature of life in those days for granted and give directions on Christian living to both slaves and their masters. St Paul taught that in Christ 'there is no longer slave or free' (Gal 3:28) and he gave a broad hint to the slave-owner Philemon that he should free his runaway slave Onesimus (Phil 15-16).

At the Last Supper Christ interpreted his death on the cross by taking a cup of wine and saying, 'This is my blood of the covenant, which is poured out for many. Truly I tell you, I will never again drink of the fruit of the vine until that day when I drink it new in the kingdom of God' (Mk 14:24-25). By his death Christ renewed God's covenant with his people and enlarged it to include the whole human family. He achieved on the cross the decisive act of establishing God's kingdom on earth. He taught us to set our hearts on the kingdom and promised that, as a consequence, all other good will come as well (Mt 6:33). God's kingdom is not of this world in the sense that its roots are divine, not human, and that its blessings transcend earthly things. But the light of God's perfect rule shines on the struggle for human dignity for the impoverished. The kingdom of justice and freedom, which is God's will for all his children, could only come about through the death of his Son by which he identified himself with the victims of human sin in all its aspects. Jesus did not merely passively suffer but, through his voluntary suffering of death, he won a freedom over the forces of evil in which all who believe in him can share. Both oppressor and oppressed need to be freed from the dehumanising forces to which they are, in different ways, in bondage. Christ provided that freedom through his atoning death which transforms both individuals and societies when it is received with obedient faith. The exploited communities of Latin America and other places can look on Christ's cross not simply as a comfort to them in their sufferings but as a source of power transforming them and the society in which they live into a foretaste, in some measure, of the kingdom of God. Similarly, we can understand the Reproaches as an encouragement to us to accept and share with others the freedom Christ won for us through his victorious death:

> I led you from slavery to freedom …
> and brought you to a land of plenty …

I gave you a royal sceptre...
but you led your Saviour to the cross.

Theories of the Atonement Brought Together

We have looked at four different ways of understanding the atonement in the light of the Reproaches – moral influence, victory, bearing the cost of sin, and liberation. By taking each in turn we were able to concentrate on its specific insight. Each way has its own integrity which must not be impaired by making one understanding dominant and forcing others to conform to that view of the atonement. But it proved impossible to separate completely the different ways since they interact and affect each other, so that together they deepen our awareness of the means of our salvation. No single theory of the atonement should be regarded as the full truth and even the sum of them still leaves our redemption from sin a mystery to the intellect though a saving truth to faith. Many other explanations have been given and some important ones such as sacrifice have not been considered here. But it may be useful to consider how these four, which seem especially to arise from examination of the Reproaches, mutually illumine one another to further our knowledge of Christ's saving work.

No one who stops to think of Christ's death can fail to be moved both by its horror and its nobility. Human sin at its worst is here exposed and God's love, in submitting to such torture from those he created, shines out from the cross on all his human children. The Reproaches bring out the horror of sin which caused Christ's suffering by listing the details of his passion. Christ's innocent suffering moves us to repentance, as expressed in the Reproaches' petition, 'Have mercy on us!', and has inspired countless people to return good for evil. The moral influence theory, while not a sufficient explanation of the atonement on its own, is an important element in the total picture. Nor is it merely one separate bit of the full truth, it takes on added significance when it is integrated with the atonement's other aspects. The love of God shown on the cross is powerful to change human hearts; it conquers evil in a radical way which the use of force cannot do. Non-violent resistance to evil, the victory of suffering love, breaks the circle of retaliation. However, to express the full dimensions of evil we need to look at the New Testament language of mighty supernatural beings ranged against God's kingdom whom Christ vanquished by his death. We can understand from human experience how the refusal to return evil for evil creates a dynamic for good, but this is only the tip of the iceberg whose hidden depths represent the mighty victory of Christ when he absorbed the full malice of Satan in his own person, suffered a real death, and in his resurrection revealed the triumph of the cross. The main emphasis in the Reproaches is on Christ's weakness and suffering, but his triumph is shown in the acclamation, 'Holy is God! Holy and strong! Holy immortal One, have mercy on us!'

Yet there was nothing 'triumphalist' about Christ's victory on the cross because it meant humiliation, pain, death and even the sense of being forsaken by God. The victory was only won through Christ putting himself alongside sinful people who are separate from God, and bearing God's righteous judgement on sin so that the world might be reconciled to God through him. True forgiveness requires sin to be fully exposed and dealt with, and only God can do that. Christ alone, absorbing in his own person the concentrated evil of the world, is shown in the Reproaches by the contrast between what God does for us and what Christ suffered for us, 'the righteous for the unrighteous' (1 Pet 3:18). But what God in Christ achieved apart from us only becomes effective for us when we participate in Christ's access to the Father. The Reproaches list God's gracious acts for his people to highlight the contrast with their treatment of the Messiah, but we argued that as all of us share in the sins which caused the cross, so we can all receive its benefits. The New Testament understands God's saving acts for Israel as foreshadowing the greater benefits Christ won for the world, and we interpreted the Reproaches' references to those acts in the light of that understanding.

'Freedom' is a prominent idea in the Reproaches, as it is in the Bible. Christ preached and inaugurated the kingdom of God on earth and this implies the fulfilment of his righteous will that all should have abundant life. The cross brings us freedom from sin in all its aspects, so the corporate and political implications of the atonement are important, as we increasingly recognise today. 'I led you from slavery to freedom ...' is a statement with far-reaching consequences for change of attitude and action as we pray 'Thy will be done on earth...' The enemies which Christ defeated on the cross include dehumanising and enslaving forces which keep individuals and communities in any kind of bondage. The attractive power of his suffering changes hearts, giving the oppressed a sense of their own value and convicting oppressors of their injustice.

Theological analysis of the atonement is a never-ending task, but no matter how far it is taken, the fact of the atonement is of much greater importance and it will always contain a dimension of mystery which cannot be captured in human concepts. Christian people throughout the centuries have found peace with God and forgiveness of their sins through their contact with the crucified Saviour, without being able to articulate precisely how the cross brings salvation. Even those who have thought most deeply about the atonement must in the end be reduced to adoration of God's suffering love at work in Christ's cross. The great merit of the Reproaches is that their theology is implicit, that they bring us face to face with the fact of the cross, and that they lead us to put our full confidence in the Saviour God revealed in Christ.

> My people, what have I done to you?
> How have I offended you? Answer me.
> *Holy is God!*
> *Holy and strong!*
> *Holy immortal One,*
> *have mercy on us!*